xBiog Magel.F Bitos.S

Bitossi, Sergio.

Ferdinand Magellan /

c1985.

❖ **Why They Became Famous** ❖

FERDINAND MAGELLAN

❖ *Why They Became Famous* ❖

FERDINAND MAGELLAN

Sergio Bitossi

Translated by Stephen Thorne

Silver Burdett Company

ACKNOWLEDGMENTS

We would like to thank Vincent Cassidy, Department of History, University of Akron and Verna Mair, Library Consultant, Aldine I.S.D., Texas for their guidance and helpful suggestions.

Library of Congress Cataloging in Publication Data

Bitossi, Sergio.
　Ferdinand Magellan.

　(Why they became famous)
　Translation of: Perchè sono diventati famosi, Magellano.
　Summary: Recounts how the sixteenth-century Portuguese explorer launched the first voyage around the world, although he met his death before his men completed the expedition.
　1. Magalhães, Fernão de, d. 1521 — Juvenile literature. 2. Explorers — Portugal — Biography. 3. Voyages around the world. [1. Magellan, Ferdinand, d. 1521. 2. Explorers. 3. Voyages around the world]

　I. Title   II. Series.
　G286.M2B58 1985   910'.924[B] [92]   84-40405
　ISBN 0-382-06854-8
　ISBN 0-382-06984-6 (Soft Cover)

© Fabbri Editori S.p.A., Milan 1982
Translated into English by Stephen Thorne for Silver Burdett Company
from Perché Sono Diventati Famosi: Magellano
First published in Italy in 1982 by Fabbri Editori S.p.A., Milan

© 1985 Silver Burdett Company. All rights reserved. Printed in the United States of America. Published simultaneously in Canada. This publication, or parts thereof, may not be reproduced in any form by photographic, electrostatic, mechanical or any other method, for any use, including information storage and retrieval, without written permission from the publisher.

CONTENTS

	Page
Ferdinand Magellan: A Restless Soldier and Sailor	5
"The World is Round, and I'll Prove It"	13
Mutinies and a Fruitless Search for the Strait	20
"The Strait! The Strait!"	31
Savage Lands and the Loss of the Leader	36
The Victoria Sails Around the World	50
Appendix	54
The Death of Ferdinand Magellan	54
Antonio Pigafeta, Magellan's Diarist	55
The Lusiads: A Poem About the Great Portuguese Navigators	56
The Diary of a Genoese Pilot	57
Historical Chronology	58

Ferdinand Magellan: A Restless Soldier and Sailor

On September 20, 1519, a small fleet of five ships set sail from the Spanish seaport of San Lucar de Barrameda under the command of Captain-General Ferdinand Magellan. The ships were the *Trinidad*, Magellan's flagship, the *San Antonio*, the *Concepcion*, the *Santiago* and the *Victoria*. About 250 men were aboard, most of them Spanish, a few Portuguese, and the rest from other countries including a gunner from England.

As an ocean breeze filled the sails and carried the ships bravely out into the Atlantic to the cheers of a crowd on the dock, nobody could foresee that the voyage would end in triumph and tragedy. None of the five captains would return. One ship would complete the voyage. She would carry 18 men, the sole survivors of the first voyage around the world.

Magellan, a Portuguese captain in command of this Spanish expedition, was an experienced sailor noted for his intelligence, boldness, and ability to command. He intended to reach the Spice Islands of the Orient by sailing across the Atlantic and through a passage into the Pacific—if such a passage existed. He felt confident that it did, and that he would find it.

Portuguese sea captains had already reached the Spice Islands—the Moluccas—by sailing east. Bartholomew Dias rounded the southern tip of Africa and sailed into the Indian Ocean in 1488. Vasco da Gama crossed the Indian Ocean to India in 1498. Lopez de Sequeira rounded India and crossed the Bay of Bengal to Malacca on the Malay Peninsula in 1509. Meanwhile, Christopher Columbus had sailed boldly across the Atlantic in 1492 and discovered the New World for Spain.

The Portuguese and the Spaniards, basing themselves on a decision of the Pope, agreed in the Treaty of Tordesillas to divide the newly discovered lands between them by drawing a line around the world from north to south. Everything east of the line went to Portugal. Everything west of the line went to Spain. The line cut through the "hump" of South America, which explains why Portuguese is spoken in Brazil today, while the rest of Latin America speaks Spanish.

But where did the Spice Islands lie with regard to the Tordesillas line as extended to the other side of the world? Nobody knew for sure because nobody knew how wide the Pacific Ocean was. The Portuguese reached the East Indies by sailing east. Magellan would reach them by sailing west. After crossing the Pacific, he would be able to locate the Indies on a map of the world, and everyone would see whether they fell within the Portuguese or the Spanish sphere of influence.

Magellan felt certain that the Spice Islands were on the Spanish side of the Tordesillas line. That was one reason why the King of Spain approved of Magellan's voyage.

But in view of the Spanish-Portuguese rivalry, it is easy to see why the Spanish captains on the voyage disliked their Portuguese commander. Some said he was really loyal to Portugal rather than to Spain. This charge was untrue. Still, it caused them to be suspicious of Magellan.

Then there were those aboardship who became doubtful when they learned that Magellan intended to do something that had never been done before. "We are going to sail around the world," he told his captains at a meeting before the departure from San Lucar. "Columbus sailed west across the Atlantic and returned to Spain. We will sail west across the Atlantic and keep going until we get home by the eastern route—past India and Africa."

While not everyone relished the idea of so dangerous a voyage, nobody deserted before it began. The men were willing to follow Magellan and see what would happen. He was an experienced sea captain—that much was certain. The Spanish captains would watch how he handled the fleet, and decide what to do later on. Such was the feeling as the five ships put out to sea.

Who was this Ferdinand Magellan? And how did it happen that he, a Portuguese, commanded a Spanish fleet?

He was probably born in Oporto in 1480. His family belonged to the lower nobility, and he became a page in the royal household of the Queen of Portugal. He served in a Portuguese expedition to India in 1505, took part in the capture of Mombasa on the coast of East Africa, and was wounded in a battle off the Malabar Coast. It is difficult to follow his movements during the next few years. He certainly fought in the naval battle

of Diu, off the coast of India, where the Portuguese gained supremacy in the Indian Ocean by defeating Egyptian and Indian fleets.

He learned the meaning of defeat when he served with the expedition of Diogo Lopez de Sequeira and the Portuguese failed to take Malacca on the Malay Peninsula. Magellan saved the life of Francisco Serrão, who became his good friend. After spending some time in Lisbon, Magellan was with the great Portuguese commander, Alfonso de Albuquerque, at the capture of Malacca in 1511. That victory gave Portugal a strong base

from which to penetrate the Moluccas, known in the West as the Spice Islands, beyond Sumatra.

Magellan distinguished himself so much in the storming of Malacca that Albuquerque made him an officer. By now Magellan knew practically everything about the sailing ships of his period. He was familiar with the charts of harbors on the shores of Africa, India, and the Malay Peninsula. He had learned the arts of war and peace in foreign lands. He knew that more of the earth's surface remained to be explored, and he hoped to be a leader of that exploration.

Magellan was ready for a command of his own. But he had to put the thought aside while serving as a subordinate in eastern waters.

In Malacca he met the people of the Malay Peninsula that extends south between Sumatra and Borneo. Their leaders often came aboard the Portuguese ships when Magellan and his companions were relaxing on deck. He learned how to deal with them when they arrived to barter spices and gold for Western bells, fishhooks, and mirrors. He liked Malaya. "Perhaps," he thought, "I can get a command that will let me explore the East Indies! I will fill the holds of my ships with pepper, cloves, cinnamon, and nutmeg! I will return triumphantly to Malacca with my cargoes from the Spice Islands!"

This was not to be. Some of the Portuguese in Malacca became jealous of him, and they persuaded Albuquerque to send him home. In any case, the year 1512 found Magellan back in Lisbon. Seeking further employment in the service of Portugal's King Manuel, he received a soldier's commission in the royal army at war in Morocco.

Those were the days when Portugal held strong points in North Africa as well as in the Far East. There was much hard fighting in Morocco. The Portuguese general needed soldiers, and Magellan was one of those who served under his command. At the Battle of Azimur, Magellan suffered another wound, a leg injury that left him with a permanent limp.

Assigned to guard some sheep, houses, and cattle captured by the Portuguese, Magellan was accused of selling a few of the animals back to the enemy and putting the money in his own pocket. Indignantly Magellan hurried to Lisbon, received a royal audience, and asked King Manuel to have the accusation withdrawn. Instead, the king ordered him to return to Morocco where the charges were being investigated. Magellan did so, and he was cleared of any wrongdoing in the case of the captured livestock. He soon returned to Lisbon to seek another post in the armed forces of the king of Portugal. He had seen enough of the army, and now he wanted a command at sea where he felt more at home. He was really a sailor at heart.

Expeditions constantly departed from Lisbon bound for Portuguese possessions abroad or for unexplored regions of the world. Sailors returned from distant lands with colorful, dramatic stories of what they had seen. Magellan wanted to do something similar himself.

Was it realistic for him to cherish this hope? He thought so when he considered how many captains less able than he were in command of fleets on the high seas.

Magellan felt that he had a right to a command of his own in view of all he had done for his king and his country. He bore on his body the scars of wounds suffered in battles in the royal service from Morocco to Malaya. He had endured the sufferings of long voyages, in storms near the Cape of Good Hope and in the blazing heat of the tropics. He had served faithfully under a number of Portuguese commanders—military men on land and captains on the high seas. Surely he deserved a promotion to captain!

Few other Portuguese sailors, and none from other lands, knew the Far East as well as he did. True, he never reached the Spice Islands, but he sailed in the East Indies, possibly landing on Sumatra, just across from Malacca, on Borneo to the east and on Java to the south. He may have been an officer on a ship that turned north into the South China Sea, which raises the possibility of his reaching China or even Japan.

Most of this is guesswork because Magellan was not the type to talk about himself. Even those closest to him, and those who admired him, knew little about his past except what they had seen for themselves. Antonio Pigafetta, the chronicler aboard Magellan's flagship on the great voyage that circumnavigated the globe, calls him "so noble a Captain" but gives no details about him apart from this voyage itself.

"Magellan's a man of few words," said one of his acquaintances. "He keeps to himself and seems to think of nothing but going to sea again. Those who have seen him in action consider him a great leader. He is afraid of nothing."

Francisco Serrão spoke in the same vein. "You saved my life when we fought together at Malacca," he wrote to Magellan. "I remember that when I fell, you beat back the Malayans with your sword. I hope the day will come when you will sail to the Spice Islands." Magellan's thoughts constantly turned toward that part of the world. He wanted to command ships in the seaborne trade. He also wanted to explore in the waters of the East Indies where the Portuguese had not yet ventured.

The second motive—exploration—was the most important for him, for he was a true son of the Age of Discovery. He longed to do something dramatic, something that would catch the attention of the world. Da Gama had sailed to India. Almeida had reached Malacca. Columbus had discovered the Americas, which were becoming better known with every expedition sent out to the New World by Portugal or Spain. Why should Ferdinand Magellan not be part of this tradition?

The map of the earth was being filled in. But there seemed to be no limit to the amount of exploration still to be done. The Far East presented an enormous area never visited by Europeans. Having been there already, Magellan believed that his best chance lay in that direction.

Besides, the wealth of the Spice Islands might attract financial backing for another voyage. The spices that arrived at Lisbon from the Moluccas paid the cost of a voyage many times over. "Yes," he said to himself, "that is the direction to go!"

"The World is Round, and I'll Prove It!"

In those days no sea captain could lead such an exploring expedition without permission from the king. The ruler of Portugal was King Manuel I, a monarch who was extremely interested in the discovery of lands that could be added to the Portuguese Empire. King Manuel had approved the voyages of da Gama, Almeida, and Albuquerque. Magellan hoped to be the next on the list.

He made his appeal when King Manuel received him at the royal Court in Lisbon in the year 1516. Manuel sat on the throne clad in royal robes, and wearing a crown on his head. Near the throne stood the king's civilian advisers and military men.

Magellan knelt before the throne. When the king asked why he was there, Magellan said he wanted to lead an expedition around Africa and India to the East Indies. He explained that he would increase Portuguese trade with the Spice Islands. He promised to look for unknown lands east of the Moluccas. He added that all this would be for the glory of Portugal and her reigning monarch.

The king listened attentively to this appeal. He knew Magellan, who had been a page for his mother, the former Queen of Portugal. He was aware that Magellan had served his country as a stalwart soldier and sailor. It would have been proper for King Manuel to approve Magellan's voyage. Turning to his chief adviser, who stood next to the throne, the king asked for an opinion.

"Your Majesty, Magellan was accused of wrongfully selling livestock captured by your troops in Morocco," said the adviser.

"Your Majesty, I was cleared of that accusation," Magellan retorted.

"That is so," the king observed.

His adviser frowned. "There was also Albuquerque's bad report on Magellan when Magellan served under Albuquerque in the Indies."

"Magellan, what do you say to that?" Manuel demanded.

"Your Majesty, my enemies out there told Albuquerque false tales about me. That was why he ordered me home to Lisbon."

"Can you prove that?" the adviser snapped.

"No," Magellan confessed. "It was just my word against theirs."

This was an honest answer, but it irritated the king. Manuel believed Portuguese commanders rather than those who served under them, and so he believed Albuquerque's report on Magellan. Also, the king disliked Magellan's attitude. Magellan was not a courtier who would bow and scrape while at court. He spoke directly to the point like the bluff sailor he was. He would not flatter the king of Portugal to curry favor.

"I have other sea captains who can sail to the East Indies," Manuel stated. "I prefer them. Magellan, your appeal is denied. You will not command a Portuguese fleet."

13

Magellan spoke slowly. "Then will your Majesty allow me to offer my services to some other country since they are not acceptable in my own?"

"Do as you please," the king retorted. "It does not matter to me where you go."

As Magellan left the palace, he felt angry because Manuel had turned him away in so insulting a manner. He also felt disappointed by the rejection of his plan for an expedition to the Far East. Gradually these feelings wore off. They were replaced by a determination to leave Portugal and seek a command at sea somewhere else.

It was common in the Age of Discovery for sea captains to represent countries other than their own. Columbus, a Genoese who sailed for Spain, was the outstanding example. In fact Columbus had tried to get backing from Portugal first. He was refused, and only then went to Spain, where he was fortunate in gaining the support of Queen Isabella.

Magellan also decided to go to Spain because it was the other great exploring nation of his time. He waited in Portugal for a year in order to regain some money he had loaned to a Lisbon businessman. During that time a dramatic new idea came to him. His idea was simply this. Instead of traveling east around Africa to the Indies, he would travel west across the Atlantic and approach them from the opposite direction. Then he would continue on around the world.

His confidence in his plan grew because of a letter from Francisco Serrão, who had abandoned a Portuguese expedition to live in the Spice Islands. According to Serrão, the Spice Islands were close to America, so that a short voyage across the Pacific would reach them. Of course Serrão was wrong, but Magellan believed him—which shows how vague they were about the size of the Pacific.

How would a ship get through the Americas from the Atlantic to the Pacific? Many geographers believed that South America extended down to the Antarctic Continent. That of course was a false idea. We know it is just as possible to sail around South America's Cape Horn as it is around South Africa's Cape of Good Hope. Magellan, however, did not know that. Nor did his friend Ruy Faleiro, a mathematician, astronomer and geographer to whom he revealed his plan.

"Magellan, what if South America extends to the South Pole?" Faleiro asked.

"Maybe it does, but that doesn't matter. There must be a strait connecting the Atlantic and the Pacific. I'll search along the coast of South America until I find it."

Faleiro became convinced that Magellan's plan to sail west to the Spice Islands was sound. Faleiro was an odd individual who talked too much and often quarreled with those who rejected his opinions. He sometimes suffered from nervous attacks that left him unable to work. Nevertheless, he was a leading expert on the way in which the map of the world was changing as new discoveries came to light. He helped Magellan with information from the newest books and charts published in centers of learning across Europe from Lisbon to Prague.

Magellan and Faleiro strolled around Lisbon discussing ways and means of gathering money, ships, and men for an expedition. They visited the waterfront to talk to sea captains just in from the high seas. Now and then Faleiro would unroll one of his maps and show Magellan where newly mentioned places were located.

Magellan, for his part, helped Faleiro with information derived from Serrão. "The Spice Islands are a paradise," wrote Magellan's friend who lived on the island of Ternate after refusing to return to Malacca, where he would again have to take orders from the Portuguese commander. "The people are charming, the climate is balmy. I am leading the pleasantest life imaginable. Why don't you join me?" While Magellan had no

intention of imitating Serrão and remaining in the Spice Islands, he felt a strong desire to see the marvels that Serrão described.

The year he spent in Portugal after his meeting with King Manuel was helpful to Magellan because it gave him time to perfect his plan. By the time he left his native land, he had a general idea of the number of ships and men he would need to put the plan into operation. In particular, the holds of the ships would have to be large enough to carry Western goods that could be bartered for the spices of the Spice Islands.

In 1517 Magellan and Faleiro went to Spain. They stayed in Seville until the following year because it took that long to get an invitation to the Spanish Court. Seville was the center of Spanish planning for transatlantic voyages. Here Magellan and Faleiro met Juan de Aranda, a member of the naval planning board who joined them as a partner after listening to Magellan's idea for a transatlantic voyage to the East Indies. Aranda was helpful because he had influence at the Court.

Magellan and Faleiro renounced their Portuguese allegiance and vowed to become faithful servants of the king of Spain. Magellan married Beatriz Barbosa, a daughter of a commander of the royal arsenal in Seville.

In 1518 Magellan, Faleiro, and Aranda went to the royal court at Valladolid far to the north of Seville. Here they were received in audience by King Charles I of Spain, who later would become the Holy Roman Emperor, Charles V. A young man, King Charles was impressed when Magellan presented to him a Malay named Enrique who had come back from Malacca with Magellan.

King Charles listened courteously as Magellan explained why he had come to Spain.

"Your Majesty, the Portuguese control the eastern route to the Indies," Magellan pointed out. "The western route lies open to Spain. I will sail it in your name."

"And what if you find the strait through South America?" Charles asked.

"I will make a short voyage across the Pacific and prove that the Spice Islands are on the Spanish side of the demarcation line agreed to by Spain and Portugal. A friend of mine who lives there, Francisco Serrão, says the Spice Islands are not far from the western shores of the Americas, which are already controlled by Spain. The islands can therefore be added to Spain's possessions in the Pacific."

"What will you do after you reach the Spice Islands?" the king inquired.

"I'll sail home to Spain by the eastern route—from the Spice Islands past India and Africa. The world's round, and I'll prove it! I'll circumnavigate the globe!"

The king agreed. "Return to Seville," he told Magellan, Faleiro, and Aranda. "It is my wish for the planning board to organize the expedition."

After thanking the king, the three men went back to Seville, where Aranda, as a member of the board, was able to prod his colleagues into acting quickly on the royal command. At that time, sailors-of-fortune were attracted to seaports at the news of a new expedition. They came from all over Europe, and even from North Africa because men who knew Arabic and African languages went along as interpreters. The 250-or-so crewmen needed for Magellan's expedition were soon assembled in Seville.

The planning board decided, with the approval of the king's overseers, that five ships would be assigned to Magellan's command. The five ships were old hulks that had to be refurbished before they could be considered seaworthy. Damaged planks in their hulls were replaced, the rigging and the sails were repaired, and the decks were cleaned. Cannon were set on carriages prepared for them with their muzzles close to the openings through which they would fire if the gunners went into action.

Magellan kept an eye on every detail as the work progressed. Having served aboard many vessels, he understood what it took to withstand the pounding of ocean waves or to ride out a storm on the ocean.

The largest of the five, the *San Antonio* at 120 tons, had Juan de Cartagena for its captain. Magellan himself was captain of the second largest, the *Trinidad* at 110 tons. The *Concepcion*, 90 tons, was under Gaspar de Quesada. The *Victoria*, 85 tons, was under Luis de Mendoza. Last came the *Santiago*, 75 tons, of Juan Rodriquez Serrano.

In spite of Magellan's attention to detail, there were vexing problems that held up the project. Sometimes supplies for the ships did not appear on time. Sometimes the repair work had to be done over. Sometimes the naval planning board objected to the cost.

The Spaniards complicated matters still further with their envious pride, and by skillful plotting succeeded in having their own man appointed commander of the ship that was second to the *Trinidad* in the fleet. Juan de Cartagena received the appointment to the *San Antonio* with broad powers over the fleet, making him Magellan's deputy and to some extent even Magellan's rival once the ships were out on the ocean.

While Magellan was doing his utmost to speed up the departure and get together everything necessary for two years at sea in the holds of his ships, his captains objected to having so many Portuguese among their crews. The captains showed a preference for Spaniards, Italians, Germans, and Flemish. In one respect Magellan profited from this feeling because the Italians included Antonio Pigafetta from Vicenza, who was to act as secretary to the commander-in-chief. This was also a stroke of great good fortune for posterity. With the shrewdness and skill of a modern "special correspondent," Pigafetta wrote of Magellan's adventures in a way that went far beyond simply listing the lands they visited and the day-to-day running of the ship.

At last the day Magellan had been waiting for arrived. The five ships raised anchor at Seville, dropped down the Guadalquiver to San Lucar de Barrameda, and, on September 20, 1519, headed out into the Atlantic.

18

Mutinies and a Fruitless Search for the Strait

From San Lucar, Magellan directed his fleet to the Canary Islands, out in the Atlantic to the southwest off the coast of Africa. The Canaries had belonged to Spain since 1479 by an agreement signed with Portugal. They were a good stopping place for Spanish expeditions, which could bring supplies aboardship before continuing on a lengthy voyage. It was here that Magellan ordered his ships to drop anchor in the harbor of Tenerife in order to restock with fresh water and meat.

The crews saw a very strange thing which, as the "miracle," was talked about for long after. Towards midday a thick cloud descended on one of the islands which had no natural springs. Almost touching the ground, the cloud settled on a huge tree whose leaves then started to drip water, which ran down the trunk to the ground. The local people obtained their water at the foot of this tree. The spectacle struck Pigafetta, who recorded it in his journal. He tells us that the water ran into a trench in such a stream that human beings and animals could drink as much as they needed every day. Pigafetta treats this as a natural scientific phenomenon, not a miracle.

Magellan's fleet continued southwest between the Cape Verde Islands and the African coast. One night, after a heavy storm, the *Trinidad* was suddenly bathed in a dazzling light—St. Elmo's fire—which quickly made the crews forget about the "rain-tree." The phenomenon, caused by certain electrical conditions in the atmosphere, is well-known to modern science, but at the time it was considered a marvel. The strange light settled on the mainmast of the flagship and remained there for more than two hours. Even Pigafetta was alarmed by St. Elmo's fire, and he was one of those who felt relieved when the sea grew calm and the fire vanished.

Magellan, however, had other things on his mind. Juan de Cartagena was already questioning his leadership. Cartagena thought Magellan was sticking too close to Africa and should be heading directly for South America. When Cartagena's *San Antonio* came close enough to Magellan's *Trinidad* for conversation, Cartagena called across that Magellan was wrong about the direction they were taking. The Spanish Captain became discourteous with the Captain-General. Each of the other four captains was supposed to salute Magellan aboard his flagship every evening. Cartagena chose to ridicule Magellan instead.

At last Magellan felt that he had no alternative to taking drastic action against his insubordinate captain. On the next occasion when all four captains came in small boats to a conference on the *Trinidad*, Magellan ordered Cartagena to be arrested.

Cartagena said to the others, "You know I'm right about our course. Stand by me, a fellow Spaniard, against this Portuguese commander. I'll take us to South America."

"We're on the right course according to my charts," Magellan retorted. "As for my plans, you will learn the details in good time."

The captains would not reject Magellan's authority. They stood aside while Cartagena was taken aboard the *Victoria* and held prisoner there. Magellan gave command of the *San Antonio* to another Spanish officer, Antonio de Coca.

The captains dispersed to their ships. The voyage resumed, with Magellan turning the prows of the ships toward South America at the point indicated by his charts.

Although the Spanish captains gave in, they were not pleased with all this, nor did they cease to criticize Magellan in the privacy of their own ships. Magellan heard rumors about this, but he did not care as long as they obeyed his orders to follow his flagship where it went. Lights on the stern of the *Trinidad* told them by night where it was, and no one could desert by pretending that he got lost in the darkness.

The fleet proceeded in this manner across the Atlantic until the lookouts in the crow's-nests atop the tallest masts caught sight of the South American coast. This was Brazil, a Portuguese territory much larger than Portugal itself. Discovered by Pedro Cabral in 1500, Brazil had not yet been settled by the Portuguese. The Spanish expedition could therefore anchor near the site of Rio de Janeiro without fear of being challenged.

"That land of Verzin (Brazil) is wealthier and larger than Spain, France, and Italy put together," Pigafetta wrote. "It belongs to the King of Portugal."

The voyage across the Atlantic had been marked by storms and the even more terrifying calms that brought sailing ships to a halt, unable to move because there was no wind to hit their sails and push them forward. Magellan was therefore pleased to order a break in the voyage so that his men could relax and get their second wind before heading south in search of a strait that would lead them through to the Pacific.

Brazil was rich in all kinds of food. Soon the ships were loaded with fruit and vegetables, two things of extreme importance in preventing scurvy, a disease that attacked the gums on extended voyages when fresh fruit and vegetables ran out. We know now, as Magellan and his contemporaries did not, that scurvy is caused by a deficiency of vitamin C.

Pigafetta set down a description of the native people of Brazil. He exaggerated their longevity, saying that they customarily lived to be 125 to 140 years old. But many of his other observations were correct. Thus, he comments that they were stone age people who did not know the use of metal. The women cultivated the fields while the men fished from canoes. Both decorated themselves with parrot feathers. "Men and women are as well proportioned as we," the Italian chronicler concluded.

The Brazilians were friendly. "They built us a house as they thought we were going to stay with them for some time, and at our departure they cut a great quantity of brazilwood to give to us." The point about brazilwood was that it produced a brilliant red dye much admired by those people. It was therefore a real gift from them to their visitors from over the sea.

Magellan remained for 13 days in the bay at Rio de Janeiro. He ordered his chaplain to say a special Mass to thank God for the safe voyage he and his men had made, and to ask devoutly for continuing divine help in their enterprise. While they were resting in that sun-drenched land, a drought of months was suddenly broken by torrential rain. The natives immediately decided that the white strangers were divine spirits and gods, and became even more generous and servile towards them.

The ships had been overhauled and given minor repairs. The holds were full of food. Magellan, who still refused to reveal his plans to the other commanders in his fleet, checked the cargo lists of his ships, ordered the anchors to be weighed, and set a course southward.

They reached the estuary of the River Plate, the meeting place of tumbling waters of the Parana and the Uruguay, on January 10, 1520. It was here that the lookouts noticed giants on the land, and called out in alarm that they could see cannibals. Rushing to the rails, the sailors did indeed see naked creatures on the beach who were extremely tall. One came on board, but the others fled from a landing party that went ashore in the hope of learning from them whether a strait existed at this point. Magellan was in a hurry to continue with his explorations, and hope urged him on. The mouth of the Plate was so wide that Magellan thought this might be the strait into the Pacific. He sailed far enough into it to be bitterly disappointed—it was only a river that became narrower upstream. Besides, the water was fresh, while a strait would hold the salt water of the oceans.

He was sailing blind. Since no explorer had ever reported finding a strait along the coast of South America, there was nothing Magellan could do but explore every indentation along the coast. He had no charts or maps to guide him. He could not afford to sail past any point that could conceivably lead to a strait.

He was also sailing on his nerve. For all the confidence in which he had begun the voyage, it seems inconceivable that he did not wonder now and then if he could be wrong. "What if I have led all these men astray?" he must have asked himself.

Yet he kept indomitably onward. He was a visionary who never lost faith in his vision. In this respect he resembled Columbus, another sea captain who refused to believe that the ideas that possessed him could be incorrect. Of course Columbus was incorrect in believing that he had reached the East Indies by sailing west. He had in fact stumbled on a New World. But then, he would not have done that if he had not followed his vision to the end.

Magellan's problem was different. He knew he had reached South America. There was no possibility of his running into a New World. The only question was whether the strait of which he dreamed actually existed. That it did was his vision. And, like Columbus, he achieved what he did because he followed that vision.

But as he kept pushing the bow of the *Trinidad* into one point on the coast after another, he could not know for sure what the outcome would be. By night he sat alone in his cabin, mulling over his problem. A religious man, he said his prayers faithfully, asking for divine support when everything human seemed to be failing him.

He knew his men were doubtful about the outcome. When he talked with them, he could sense their skepticism. He could also see how his own spirit encouraged them. "We have all come this far together," he exhorted them. "Let us go on together."

But the coastline continued without a break, and enthusiasm began to wane. League after league, the fleet continued on its way towards the Antarctic amid islands inhabited

by vast numbers of penguins. The ships were again short of fresh meat, and the sailors caught penguins by the dozen, skinning them even before removing their feathers. Hunger was bad, but the cold was worse—freezing winds continually swept the decks of the ships and carried stinging sleet and snowflakes with them.

   Here and there the men saw gigantic icebergs floating on the waves, and the helmsmen were often hard put to avoid them. The solid gray sky lowered over them like a funeral shroud. To avoid the worst, Magellan looked for an inlet where he could ride out the winter, and on March 31, 1520, at 49° latitude south, he ordered his captains to drop anchor in the Bay of San Julian. There they saw a nearly nude man of great height who, on seeing the sailors landing, began to dance and sing and throw dust on his head as if he had been seized by some sort of frenzy. His face was painted red, his eyes were ringed with yellow and two hearts were painted right in the middle of his cheeks. His hair was dyed white, and his only garment was a moth-eaten skin. When a mirror was placed before him and he saw his reflection, he leapt backwards in an almost comical way and nearly fell flat on the sand. Everyone laughed. Magellan watched their hilarity and interpreted it as a good sign.

   "We'll winter here," he informed his captains.

Once they had gotten over their fear of the white men from the sea, the natives became trusting and approached the sailors' campfires, showing their desire for friendship and hospitality. Indeed, one of the bolder, or perhaps more reckless, of the tribe went so far as to be baptized a Christian and accept the name of John. He learned how to say Jesus and the Virgin Mary in Spanish. Not all of Magellan's men were quick to appreciate the hospitality they had been shown, and one of them was caught by the natives while trying to harm some of them. A Spaniard was shot in the thigh by an arrow and died of the infection, and some of the natives were killed by the sailors' muskets. Others were captured and put in irons in the holds of the ships.

These were minor incidents compared to other things that occurred in San Julian Bay. It was here that the resentment of the Spanish captains burst into a mutiny against Magellan. He was in danger of losing not only his command but his life as well.

The old suspicion of Magellan flared up as the fleet sailed south along the South American shore into the region of savages, ice floes, and penguins. Heavy gales tore at the sails. The Antarctic weather chilled officers and men to the bone—they had never expected to be this far south, and the clothing they brought with them was inadequate in the frigid climate they were pushing through. The voyage was behind schedule. By now they should have been through the strait into the Pacific.

But was there any strait? That question became more frequent when the Spanish captains conferred behind Magellan's back. They wondered if he was really searching for a strait. "Is our commander intending to betray us?" they asked. "Is he hoping that our four ships will be lost, after which he will sail his flagship to Portugal, rather than to Spain? If he is not conspiring against us, why does he remain so silent?"

Of course that silence was caused by Magellan's bewilderment. He still believed in the existence of a strait, but he could not understand why he had come so far south without finding it. He was not involved in any conspiracy against his captains. It was just the other way around. They were conspiring against him.

The mutiny erupted on April 1 (April Fool's Day), when rebels from the *Concepcion* boarded the *San Antonio* from a small boat. Juan de Cartagena, who had been liberated from his confinement, seems to have been their leader—Cartagena, who had defied Magellan at sea and was defying him for a second time. This rebel, who had sailed from San Lucar as Magellan's deputy, was an obvious choice for commander of the fleet should Magellan be deposed.

The mutineers took over the *San Antonio*. Those aboard the *Victoria* murdered the captain and joined the uprising. There were shouts from the rebel ships. "Death to Magellan! Long live Cartagena!" The words must have pleased Cartagena, who felt he now had the upper hand. Three ships—the *Concepcion*, the *San Antonio* and the *Victoria*—were on his side. Only two, the *Trinidad* and the *Santiago*, remained loyal.

But the loyalists had Magellan on their side. The iron-willed commander called on the mutineers to surrender. He sent men across the waves in small boats to enforce his orders. As a result, the mutineers began to lose their nerve. Magellan's supporters took over the *Victoria*, which gave the commander three ships against two. When he threatened to bombard those two with his cannon, the *San Antonio* and the *Concepcion* surrendered.

Happily Magellan announced that the mutiny was over. His authority over his fleet was restored. He had given everybody aboardship an example of how a strong leader can control the most desperate situation.

The mutineers remained to be dealt with. Magellan allowed most of the men to go free. "You were misled by the ringleaders," he told them in announcing his decision. "Return to your duties aboardship, and you will have nothing to fear."

He treated two of the mutineers differently. One of the ringleaders, Gaspar Quesada, Captain of the *Concepcion*, was found guilty of murder and sentenced to death. He was decapitated on the deck of the *Trinidad*. It seemed fitting to Magellan that his flagship should be the place where just punishment was meted out to the murderer.

A different fate awaited Juan de Cartagena. He had not committed murder, but he had been the leading mutineer. As a result, Cartagena was marooned on a deserted island with a priest who had joined him in the mutiny. Food and wine were left for the two men, and the fleet sailed away leaving them to their fate. They were never heard from again. Both must have perished on their frozen island off Patagonia.

With order restored aboard his fleet, Magellan resumed his search for the elusive strait. At one point he ordered the captain of the *Santiago* to make a special search at what appeared to be a likely place. However, the ship was overwhelmed by a storm and wrecked near Cape Santa Cruz. The men aboard her were saved. They were split up among the other vessels of the fleet.

One ship of the five that set out from San Lucar was gone. The remaining four went on. No matter what happened, Magellan was not going to be stopped. His control of the mutineers gave him added confidence which was reflected by the obedience his sailors and officers gave him.

"They won't rebel again," Magellan said to one of his officers aboard the *Trinidad*. "They trust me now. I want to show that their trust is justified."

And he did.

"The Strait! The Strait!"

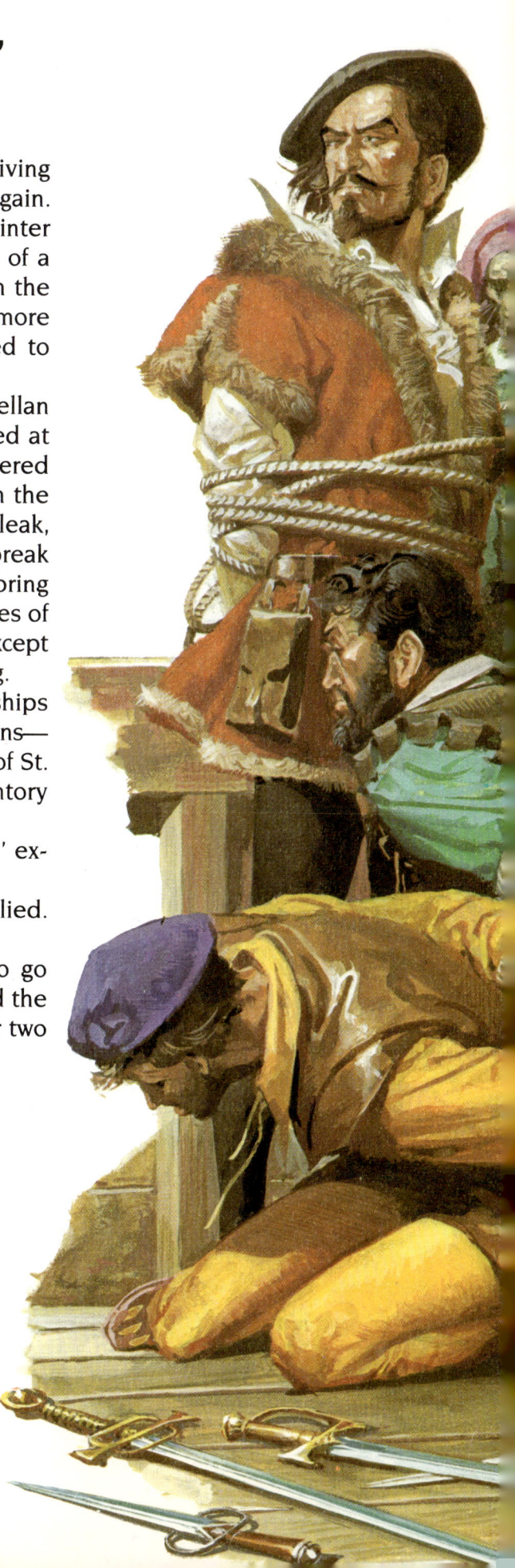

On August 24, 1520, Magellan ordered his four surviving ships to head for the open sea and then turn south again. Since he was far below the Equator, this was a winter month. However, he hoped for a speedy discovery of a passage that would enable him to sail through from the Atlantic to the Pacific, and then turn north to a more hospitable climate. Failing that, he was determined to sail on south until he did find the strait.

Moving to the area off the Rio Santa Cruz, Magellan brought his fleet to another halt. The ships remained at anchor here for two months. Once again the crews suffered not only from icy cold and high winds but also from the fear of being so near to the South Pole. Only a bleak, barren land met their eyes as they strove to see a break in the coastline. They sent landing parties ashore to bring back fresh water and wood. They fished over the sides of their ships. Otherwise, there was little they could do except hope that their commander knew what he was doing.

Again Magellan gave the order to move south. The ships rounded the promontory of the Eleven Thousand Virgins—so-called by Magellan because it was the feast day of St. Ursula and her crowd of martyrs. Beyond the promontory a broad bay extended in an arc from north to south.

"How often have we explored bays like this one!" exclaimed an officer of the *Trinidad*.

"Well, we must explore here, too!" Magellan replied. "The strait might be just in front of us!"

He ordered the *San Antonio* and the *Concepcion* to go ahead and see what they could find. The *Trinidad* and the *Victoria* waited for them to return. The wait lasted for two days.

It was a nerve-racking time. The men of the *Trinidad* and the *Victoria* occupied themselves as best they could. They talked about their predicament, or played cards, or dropped lines into the water to catch fish. Magellan spent most of the first day in his cabin mulling over his plans if this bay should prove to be one more disappointment. On the second day he prowled the deck of his flagship, stopping every now-and-then to shade his eyes with his hand, and to peer across the water toward the place where his two exploring ships had dropped out of sight.

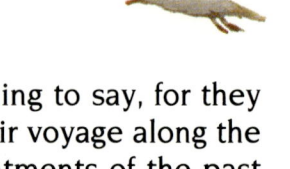

Officers and crew fell silent as he passed. There was really nothing to say, for they knew he was hoping for the strait that had not yet appeared in their voyage along the coast. And he knew they were thinking about the many disappointments of the past few months.

Marine birds wheeled overhead making harsh cries. The waves of the bay lapped against the sides of the ships. There was no other sound except the voices of the men speaking in low tones to one another or the occasional shouted command of an officer to his crew.

The silence was suddenly broken by the sound of cannon shots echoing across the bay. The *San Antonio* and the *Concepcion* hove in sight. The men of the *Trinidad* and the *Victoria* rushed to the sides of their ships or climbed into the rigging for a better view. Magellan stood on the highest deck, his hands clutching the railing.

On and on came the *San Antonio* and the *Concepcion*. Again they fired their big guns. The roar thundered across the bay in waves that died away over the land.

At last the two exploring ships were near enough for the *Concepcion's* lookout in the crow's-nest to be heard.

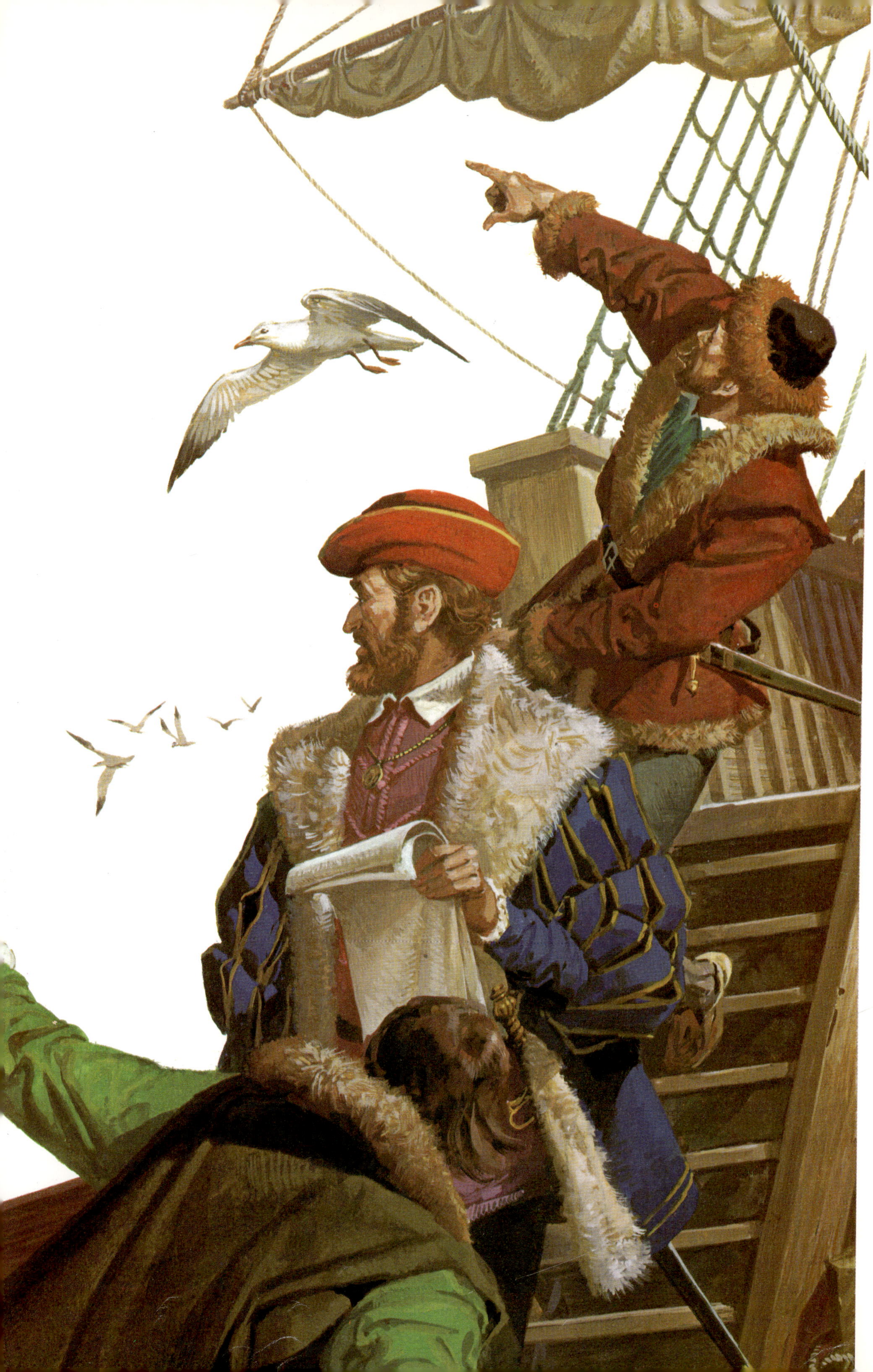

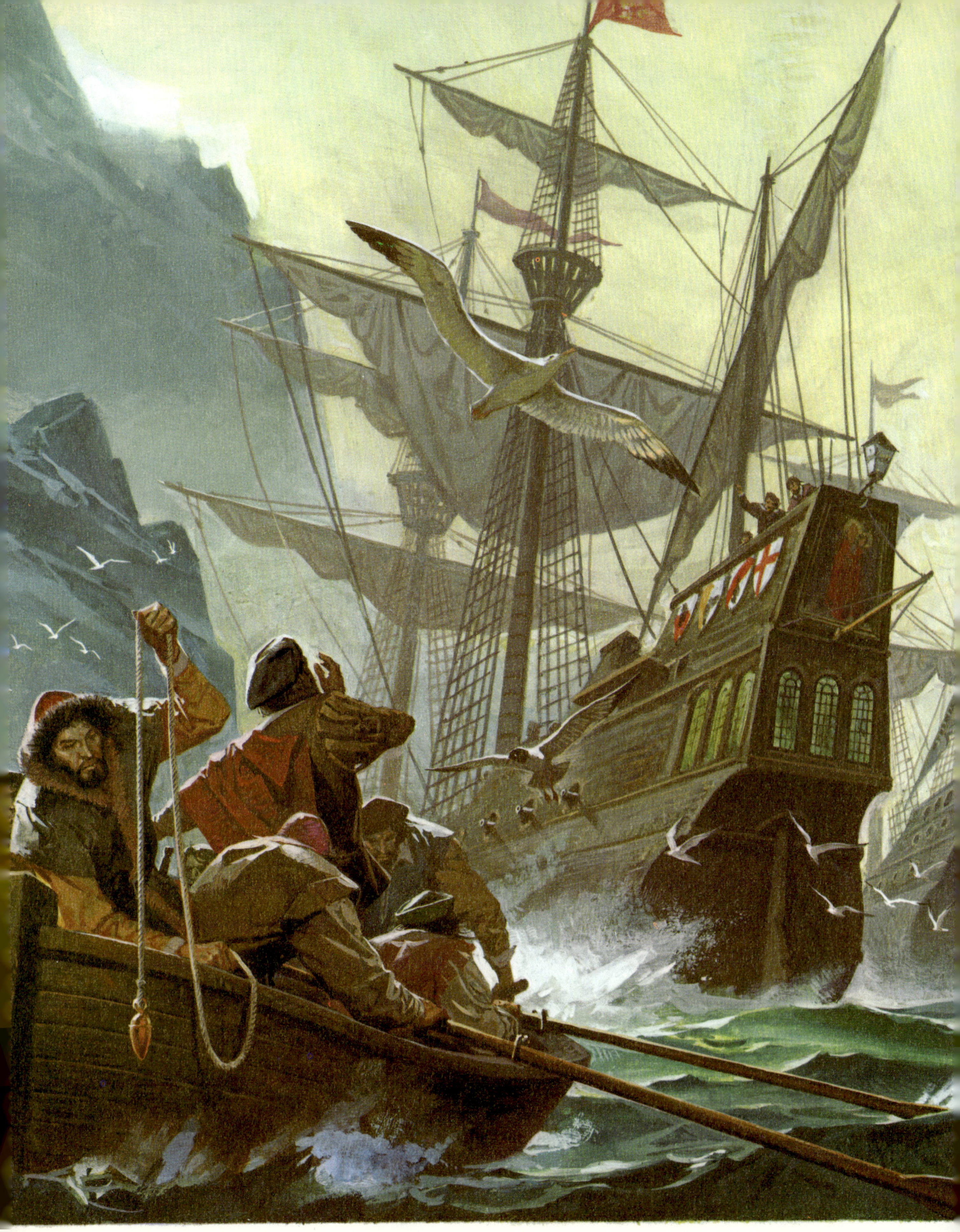

"The strait!" he yelled. "The strait! We've found it!"

A triumphant cheer went up from those aboard the ships that had been left behind. The two returning captains came aboard the flagship and reported to Magellan.

"We only got part way in," the captain of the *Concepcion* explained, "but there is a strait, not a river. The water is salty as the sea. It must come from the sea."

Magellan at once ordered his ships into the strait. "Forward! Forward!" he shouted. "This is what we have been waiting for! Success at last!"

The fleet moved forward between overhanging cliffs on one side and rocks and reefs on the other. The last thing Magellan wanted was to lose another ship as he had lost the *Santiago*. Finally, all four were safely inside the strait. It took over a month to navigate the passage, which turned out to be more than 300 miles long. In some places it was 15 miles wide.

At one point they came to two openings divided by an island in the strait. Magellan ordered the captains of the *San Antonio* and the *Concepcion* to explore one of the openings, while the *Trinidad* and the *Victoria* explored the second. The first two vessels were away so long that Magellan lowered anchor to let them catch up.

He called the region "Tierra del Fuego" ("Land of Fire") because flames were seen by night along the shores. The primitive natives who lived there did not know how to make fires. Their original fires came from lightning striking the trees, and the natives kept the fires going all the time. They were afraid of being left in cold and darkness if the fires went out.

Magellan sent a small boat ahead to explore the strait. Three days later the boat returned, and the men aboard reported that they had passed a cape from which the sea extended beyond the horizon. After so many failures—victory! It was the ocean west of the Americas! Even the iron-willed Magellan broke down and wept at the news.

The *Concepcion* rejoined the fleet. Nothing, however, was heard from the *San Antonio*. After waiting as long as he could for his missing ship, Magellan went on without it. The truth was that the *San Antonio* had deserted. A band of mutineers overpowered the captain and those loyal to him, turned the ship around, and sailed back across the Atlantic to Spain. It was well for Magellan's peace of mind that he did not know this. He would not have understood how another rebellion against him could occur just when the discovery of the strait had proved him right.

Antonio Pigafetta says Magellan named it the "Strait of Patagonia." We know it as the "Strait of Magellan." The name of the great discoverer is also on the map of the heavens. He and his men noticed two clusters of stars that are now called the "Magellanic Clouds" of the southern hemisphere.

Reduced to three ships—the *Trinidad*, the *Concepcion* and the *Victoria*—the fleet went through the strait and entered the western ocean. The surface was so smooth that Magellan called it the "Pacific Ocean." The next leg of the voyage took him north along the coast of South America, pushed by the Humboldt Current. After 900 miles, he veered west for the Spice Islands.

"This will be a short sail," he said when he brought his two remaining captains aboard his flagship for a conference. "My friend, Francisco Serrão, lives in the Spice Islands. He has written to me. And he says the Moluccas are not far from the western shore of the Americas. The worst is over for us."

Savage Lands and the Loss of the Leader

As Pigafetta noted scrupulously in his diary, the ships sailed for three months and twenty days under a pale sky by day and by the cold light of the five stars of the Southern Cross by night, without ever sighting land and "with no relief or refreshment of any kind." On board the ships the situation worsened daily, and in the end became desperate. The crews' biscuit rations were no longer worthy of the name, but stinking handfuls of rat-gnawed dust. The drinking water had gone foul in the barrels, and those who suffered most from hunger were eating the leather fittings on the rigging after soaking them in salt water for a few days to make them softer. A roasted mouse was worth a fortune.

There was also scurvy aboardship. "But above all other misfortunes," wrote Pigafetta, "the following was the worst. The gums of both the lower and upper teeth of some of our men swelled, so that they could not eat under any circumstances and therefore died. Nineteen men died from that sickness, and the giant together with an Indian from the country of Verzin. Twenty-five or thirty men fell sick in the arms, legs, or in another place, so that few remained well. However, I, by the grace of God, suffered no sickness."

At last, on March 6, 1521, land was sighted from the crow's-nests. The shout rang out: "Land ho! Land ho! God be praised!"

The words galvanized all those down below. Their thoughts were of going ashore and finding food and water. But what they came to were a couple of desert islands. Almost in despair they realized that there was no point in stopping. Magellan kept his disappointment to himself, and ordered his ships to by-pass the "Unfortunate Islands," as he appropriately called them.

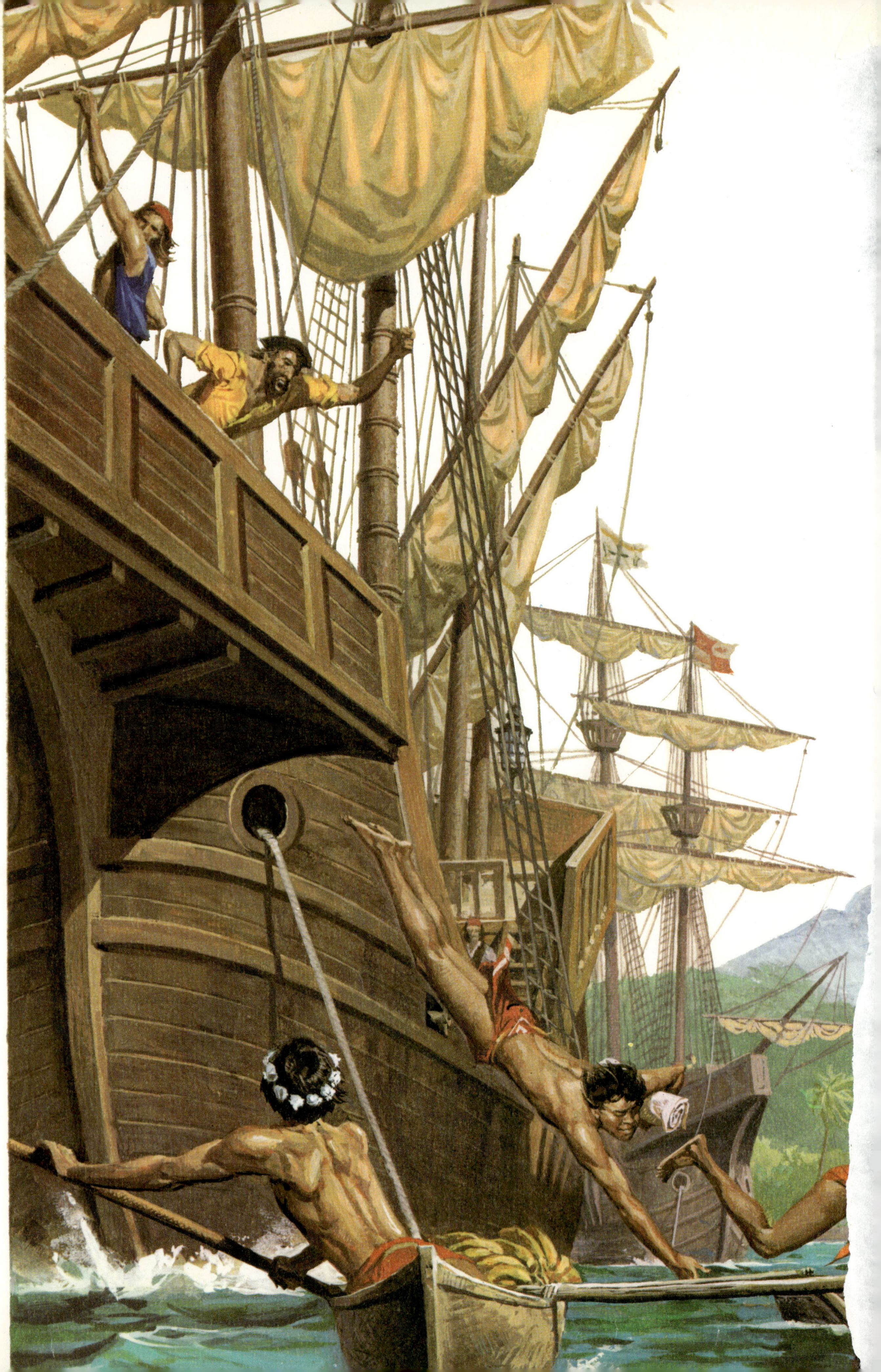

There has been much speculation about these islands. The leading theory is that they were in the Paumotu Archipelago.

Continuing on, the fleet caught the Pacific winds in their sails and drove westward until it came to a group of inhabited islands. These were the Marianas, of which Guam was the largest.

Magellan breathed a great sigh of relief. He had never expected his Pacific voyage to take so long. He realized that Serrão was wrong—the Spice Islands did not lie close to the Americas. They were on the far side of an enormous ocean. It was good to see inhabited islands.

Still, he and his men approached with great care, not knowing what they would find. They were right to do so because the islands were inhabited by real thieves, a race of malicious savages who with great boldness, and mainly at night, would glide up to the ships in their canoes, creep on board and make off with whatever they could lay their hands on, unless it were actually nailed down to the ship. They seemed like greedy animals, and they even went so far as to carry off the lifeboat of the *Victoria*.

Magellan had had enough—quite apart from the fact that it was dangerous for a ship to lose a lifeboat before putting out to sea again. He landed with a band of his men armed with muskets, repossessed what had been stolen, burned down the natives' huts, and killed seven of them in a skirmish. The climate of the "Islands of Thieves" (as the Portuguese rightly named the islands) was not particularly healthy, and they were obviously not the Moluccas. And so, having taken essential supplies on board, Magellan sailed for another three hundred leagues until he came to what is now called Samar in the Philippines.

The sailors saw men and women on the beach. Since Magellan did not know if they would be friendly or hostile, and remembering his bad experience with the thieves of the Marianas, Magellan decided not to land on Samar. Instead, he chose an uninhabited island where his men could recuperate without being harassed. Many of them were sick or exhausted from the rigors of the voyage across the Pacific. They all needed a break.

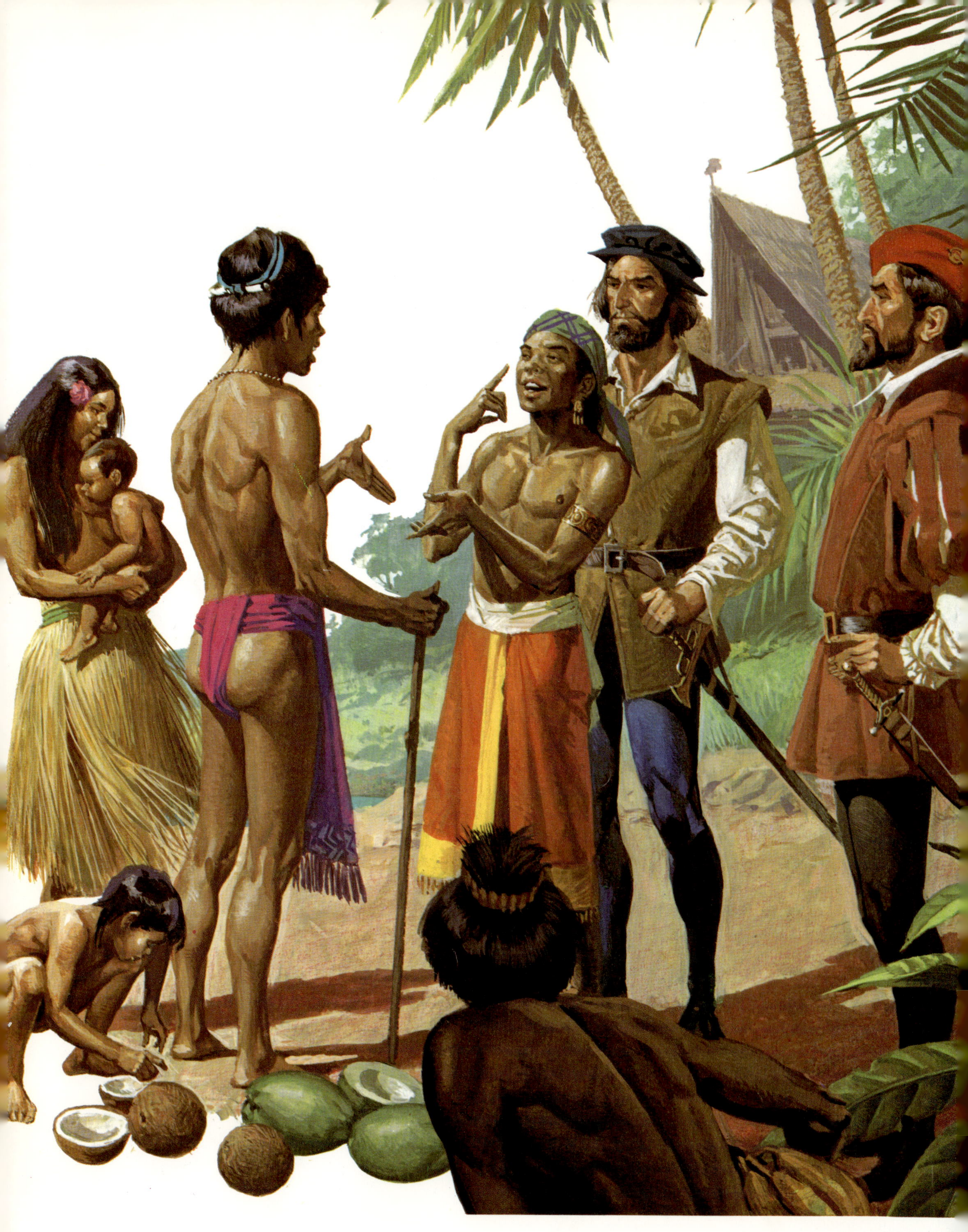

Two tents were set up for the ill, who were taken ashore from the ships. Each day for over a week Magellan came to see how they were.

On the second day, nine visitors crossed from the neighboring island of Homonhon. They were friendly, to Magellan's relief. Later they returned with coconuts, oranges, poultry, and palm wine. Between the fresh food and the chance to rest and sleep, his men were soon back on their feet. He decided to explore this archipelago, which he and his men were the first Europeans to see—the Philippine Islands.

It is impossible to tell from Pigafetta's account exactly which islands they passed or stopped at. After all, these islands were not on any European map. The Italian chronicler often could not be sure where he was, and had to guess how the islands were related to one another. But a few places can be identified under their modern names.

Magellan found that the natives were also very hospitable at Butuan and Galagan, natural harbors on the island of Mindanao. The sailors took advantage of this to exchange their assorted trinkets for spices, hens, coconuts and even nuggets of gold.

Magellan had given the strictest orders that no incident was to disturb the friendship and trust of those olive-skinned, well-fed people dressed in loin-cloths and perfumed with ointments. They all wore heavy earrings and precious bracelets, and carried daggers and knives at their waists and gleaming gold swords and heavy shields in their hands. They didn't seem warlike, however, and spent their time fishing, which they did with great skill from boats using harpoons and nets.

"No one should risk offending them," Magellan and his officers repeated to the crews. The admiral intended to establish the islands as a secure, well-protected base for Spanish ships approaching the Moluccas. He also decided, therefore, to secure the friendship of the local king who, as Pigafetta noted in great detail, came to visit Magellan on Good Friday "accompanied by eight men all in one boat. Coming on board, he embraced the captain and gave him three porcelain pots covered in leaves which contained rice, two big yellow fish, and many other things."

Magellan also offered gifts to the king—a red and yellow garment—and presented his men with knives and mirrors. He offered them a meal on board and, through an interpreter, expressed his desire to be a "casi casi," or brother, of the King. He then showed him the weaponry of the ship, and fired a cannon to satisfy their curiosity. As Ulysses had done at the court of Alcinous, in the *Odyssey*, he recounted through an interpreter his amazing voyage. His eyes filled with tears of nostalgia and with joy when he talked about discovering the strait.

The king was also moved, and he readily agreed that two members of the crew should accompany him to his hut—it goes without saying that Pigafetta was one of them, and he has left us an exact account of everything that happened on the island during the following two days.

An interesting change came over Magellan in the Philippine Islands. He showed that he wanted to be a missionary as well as a discoverer. A faithful son of the Catholic Church, he had not been particularly interested in spreading its doctrine earlier in the voyage—not in Patagonia or the Marianas, for example. The people of the Philippine Islands appear to have brought to the surface a profound religious feeling in his character. Perhaps their friendliness made him believe that they were open to conversion.

Whatever the reason, the blunt sea captain made himself responsible for the souls of the local king and his people. He invited them to Mass on Easter, returned their gestures of peace, offered to defend them from their enemies, and with the help of the chaplain succeeded in extracting a promise from the king to convert himself to Christianity, which he did directly. Standing near the cross with Magellan and mingling his voice with those of the sailors in the choir, the king devoutly recited the Pater Noster and the Ave Maria. He was then baptized together with his wife, courtiers, and about eight hundred subjects, both men and women.

In the name of God and the king of Spain, Magellan established peaceful relations with other tribes in the archipelago, and especially with the king of the island of Cebu, where he stopped to take on fresh water and food before setting out for the Moluccas. In order to impress the people, he approached the island with flags flying and cannons firing, almost like some thundering god. The king was terrified, but managed nonetheless to tell the Portuguese in no uncertain terms, through an interpreter, that in order to disembark and collect supplies he would have to pay a tribute, as did everyone else without exception.

"The king of Spain pays tribute to no man," declared Magellan, who had confidence in his guns.

"Tell your king," he instructed the interpreter, "that we come in peace and not in war, but if he wants war, he shall have fire and destruction!"

It was a tense moment, but the king was still shaken to see the smoking mouths of the cannons, and promised supplies, tributes, and the conversion of his people to Christianity. Gifts were exchanged as a sign of peace, and Magellan at last went on land with an escort to visit the king, while his sailors unloaded all their knick-knacks, set up a sort of market, and exchanged pearls and mirrors of little value for rice, pigs, goats and, above all, gold. The sailors were shrewd, and made fortunes from the people. Magellan took no part in all this; in the name of God and King Charles, he was more concerned with making the local king and his tribe love God and show proper respect for the king of Spain. On Sunday, April 14, the inhabitants of Cebu burned all their idols in front of a large iron cross and were baptized by the chaplain.

Both chiefs of the nearby island of Mactan, Zula and Silapulapu, were adamant in their refusal to accept the Gospel and swear loyalty to the king of Spain. They decided to lead Magellan into a trap. They would entice him ashore and then overwhelm him and the men he brought with him. They baited the trap by sending a messenger to declare that Zula was prepared to become a Christian and pay the tribute, except that he feared reprisals from Silapulapu. The treacherous messenger added:

"Come, then, foreigner, with your weapons. And come soon. Come to our island and help us to conquer Silapulapu. We will be very grateful if you liberate us from that terrible man, and Zula will throw himself at your feet and declare himself ready to be baptized in the name of your God. One boatload of your armed sailors will be enough because we will join you."

Magellan fell into the trap because he was anxious to teach the rebels of Mactan a lesson. He agreed to the proposal, promised armed assistance, and went ashore with sixty armed men in three boats. He thought the extra two boats would guarantee success.

"Not you!" his officers said to him when they saw him arming himself. "You stay on board!"

He was too precious to them, and fearful that a fight would break out with the natives, no one wanted him to leave. But Magellan, as always, was stubborn and courageous, and answered them in no uncertain terms.

"Perhaps the shepherd should abandon his flock when there is a wolf nearby?"

So he went, little knowing that death awaited him on the beach at Mactan.

At midnight, with a starless sky and a sea as smooth as glass, they put out from the ships lying at anchor. They shouted farewells to those who were left on board. Not one of them, well protected as they all were from their breastplates to their visored helmets, feared any personal injury. They were armed with swords, spears and daggers, and many were carrying muskets.

"Farewell!" somebody called from one of the departing boats.

"Good hunting!" came the reply from the railing above.

There were natives among the men in the boats—a recently converted king and important couriers from his tribe. They smiled without understanding what they were being asked, and pointing towards Mactan, chanted one of their dirges.

By dint of strong rowing, the boats reached the shore at three o'clock in the morning, but could not run up onto the land because the seabed was covered with jagged rocks at the water's edge. There was the risk of tearing out the bottoms of the boats. In any case, Magellan was in no hurry, and before attacking decided to deliver another ultimatum to Silapulapu.

He sent an islander, who knew the local language, to speak to those on the shore. They had been aroused by their sentinels and knew that the invaders were near. The messenger advised them to offer no further resistance, to honor the king of Spain and pay the tribute—provisions that were needed to continue the voyage to the Moluccas in comfort and safety.

One may imagine the scene on the shore in the dim light of predawn. All the warriors of Mactan, including those of Zula, were assembled with their weapons. They were in an ugly mood, for Silapulapu had addressed them in fiery words, telling them that their freedom would be gone if they submitted to the foreigners. Silapulapu listened to the messenger while his followers murmured threats.

The messenger reminded him how well-armed the Europeans were. Silapulapu replied sharply. "If you have spears that cut well, and armor, and guns, we have spears and knives that bring death to our enemies!"

"Is that your reply to our warning?"

"Yes, it is. Go back and tell your master what I have said."

The messenger did so.

Magellan had hoped that force would be unnecessary. But this was a challenge, and he could not avoid it. Waiting for dawn to break, he leaped into the water and waded toward the shore at the head of his men. There was still a chance of a peaceful outcome if Zula and his force came, as promised, to the aid of the Europeans. Perhaps Silapulapu would be cowed by the numbers arrayed against him.

A nasty surprise awaited Magellan as he got close enough to see who was on the shore. Silapulapu and Zula, the traitor, were together. Behind them there were 1,500 excited warriors ready for battle, outnumbering Magellan's force many times over. Magellan was not the type to go back just because it was dangerous to go forward. He

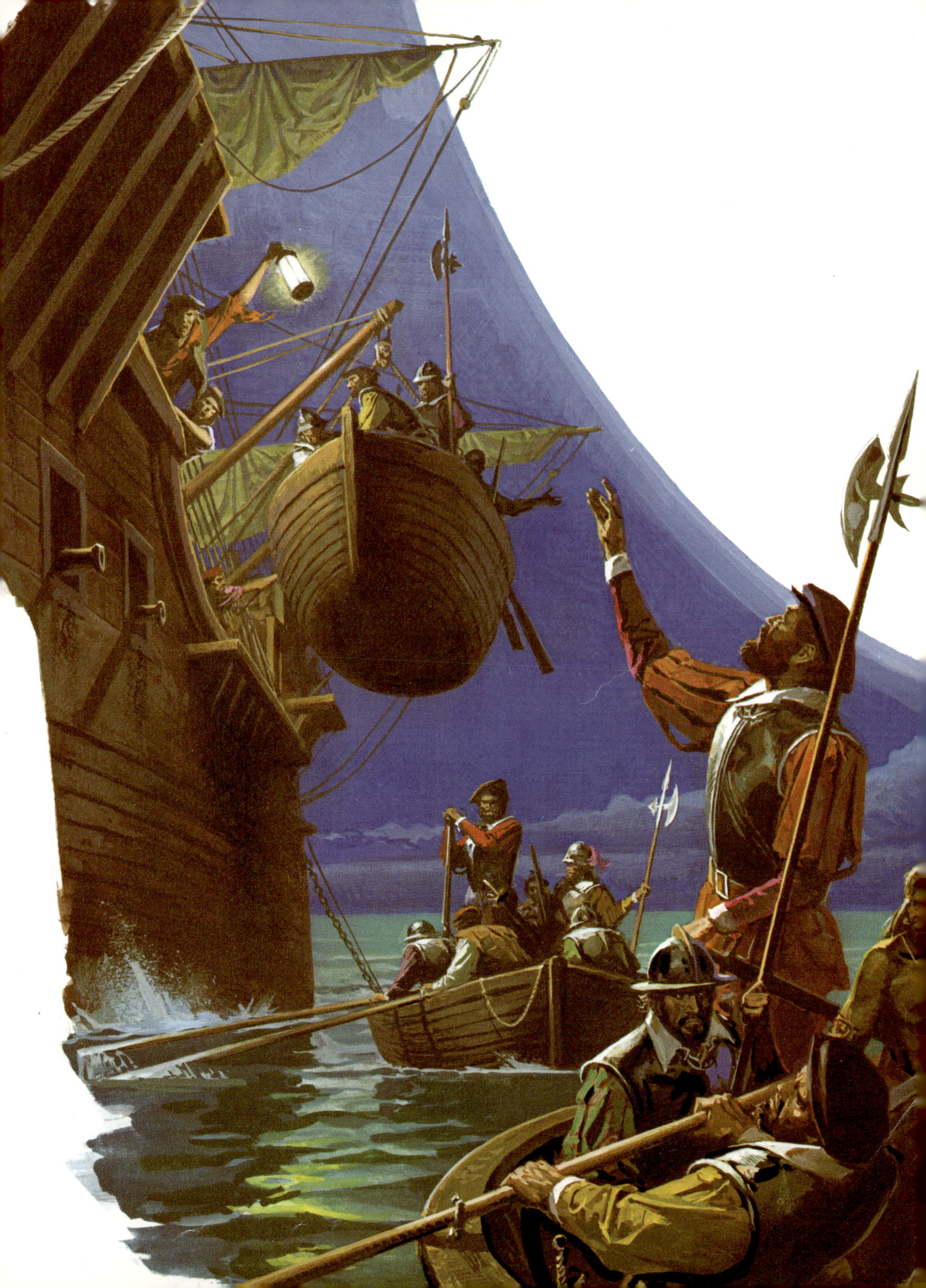

was determined to settle the issue at once.

A battle broke out in which spears and knives flew through the air. Magellan's crossbows and muskets answered in kind. The islanders had the best of the exchange because their missiles rained down in tremendous numbers. Also, Magellan and his men were wading through the water, which left them vulnerable to attack.

A wild melee broke out in the shallow water and along the beach. The Mactans showed that they were acquainted with this type of warfare, which they waged against other islands near them. They expertly aimed at the faces of the Europeans, which were exposed beneath their metal helmets. And they used their spears skillfully to ward off the knives and pikes of the enemy.

The muskets, which won so many battles for Europeans against native people around the world, were nearly useless in this battle. While in the water, the gunners could not get the footing they needed to shoot straight. By the time they reached the shore, so many were wounded that they could not handle their weapons.

When Magellan saw what was happening, he ordered some of his men to set fire to the town of the Mactans. His strategy was to demoralize them and send them fleeing back to save their burning houses. His strategy backfired, for Silapulapu used the sight to inspire his followers.

Magellan's messenger heard the Mactan chief shout: "They are destroying your houses! Make them pay for it! Kill! Kill!"

They obeyed him, attacking with greater ferocity. The islanders pushed forward. The Europeans were forced to retreat.

By now Silapulapu could identify Magellan—the man in front who was wielding his sword right and left, and shouting orders at the same time.

Silapulapu pointed at Magellan. "He is their leader! Do not let him escape!"

With victory out of the question, Magellan thought only of saving his men. He ordered a retreat to the small boats that would take them to the ships. The Mactans, under the urging of their chief, made a rush for him. They wounded him repeatedly in the face, and he fell. His companions ran to his aid, but he warned them off.

"Quick, run for it! Save your lives! That's an order!" he gasped.

He already had the faint voice and pallid features of a man close to death. Fighting for their own lives, they could not carry him off. There was no alternative. Battered and limping, they waded to the boats and escaped. They left nine dead companions, and four islanders who had come with them.

Seeing that Magellan had fallen, the Mactans stabbed him again and again. Death came to the great discoverer on April 27, 1521.

For him, the voyage was over. The resolute sea captain had led his fleet through some of the worst hardships ever endured by an expedition during the Age of Discovery. He had followed his vision of a strait between the Atlantic and the Pacific until he found it. He had endured Antarctic weather at the tip of South America, and near starvation in the middle of the Pacific Ocean. He had kept on course from Spain to islands on the opposite side of the globe. He had discovered the Marianas and the Philippines. He knew where to look for the Moluccas, the fabled Spice Islands.

And then he died on a small island, at the hands of a fierce, but proud people! Fate has rarely played a crueler trick on a great human being.

Even Silapulapu seems to have had an inkling of this. The men aboard Magellan's ships, appalled at what had happened to him, offered to buy his body for some of the goods they carried. The Mactan chief refused because he knew Magellan's worth, and was afraid his death might be denied by his officers while voyaging in the east.

That's why, to this day, nobody knows what became of the earthly remains of Ferdinand Magellan.

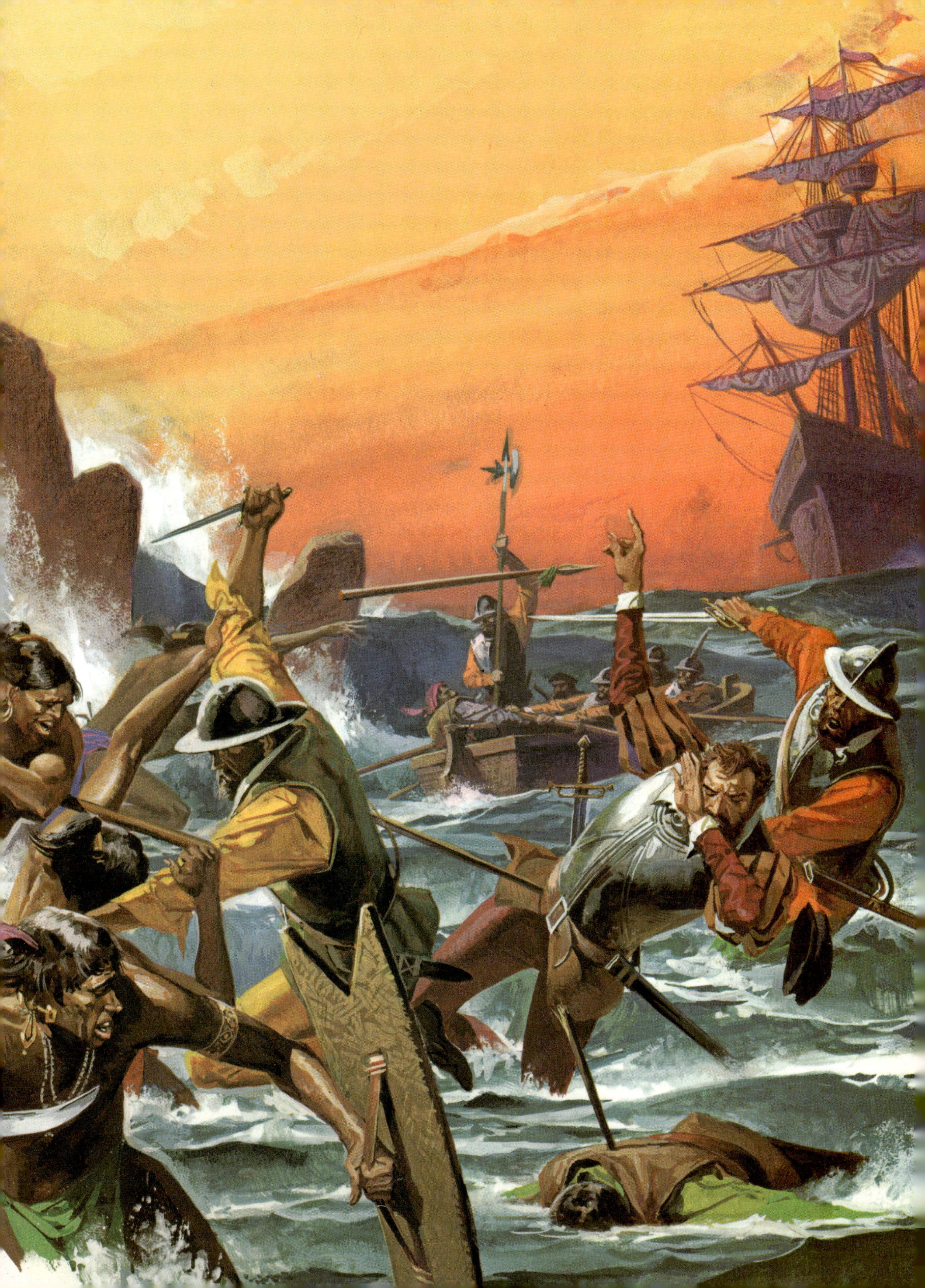

The Victoria Sails Around the World

The death of their leader threw his followers into a turmoil. They decided to sail away from Cebu after hearing that a shore party had been massacred, abandoning one man who ran to the beach and begged to be taken aboard. The *Trinidad*, the *Concepcion*, and the *Victoria* were left from the original fleet, but there were not enough of the crew to man them all. The *Concepcion*, the least seaworthy, was sacrificed—burned after everything salvageable had been removed.

The remaining two ships, under their captains, sailed through the Philippines and on to Borneo. Landing in numerous places, the Europeans met the inhabitants and on Borneo were impressed by what they saw. Pigafetta describes Brunei as a brilliant city with a large palace and a Rajah who ruled in splendor.

Finally the two ships reached their true destination—the Spice Islands. All on board felt exhilarated as they sailed into the harbor at Tidore and dropped anchor. The local people were only too eager to trade their spices for the goods brought by the Europeans. While there, Magellan's men discovered that his friend, Francisco Serrão, was dead.

As the holds of the two ships were being filled with spices, the *Trinidad* sprang a leak. She had to be left behind for repairs. It was decided that her crew would sail across the Pacific to Spanish America, which seemed an easier voyage than an attempt to follow the *Victoria* on east around India and Africa to Spain.

Actually, the Pacific voyage proved impossible. The *Trinidad* had trouble almost from the moment she got out of sight of land. Her captain did not know the route to follow in order to take advantage of the trade winds. As a result, his ship wallowed in the water, unable to make headway against winds blowing in the wrong direction. Running out of provisions, he had to turn back. He and his men were captured by a Portuguese force based in Ternate.

The Portuguese regarded the Spaniards as interlopers who had no right in the Spice Islands. Ironically, Magellan had proved they were right. The Moluccas fell on the Portuguese side of the demarcation line agreed to in the Treaty of Tordesillas. By discovering how wide the Pacific was, he disproved the statement of Francisco Serrão that the Spice Islands were close to Spanish America.

The Portuguese imprisoned the men of the *Trinidad*, most of whom disappeared from history. Some died in prison, others after they were set free. Some decided to stay in the islands rather than return home. Only four members of the crew returned to Spain.

So did the *Trinidad* disappear from history. She may have gone to the bottom in another attempt to make her seaworthy. Or, she may have been broken up by the Portuguese in order to make use of the timber, cord, and navigational instruments.

It was a sad ending for one of the most memorable ships ever to sail the seas. Fate would have been kinder to let the *Trinidad* rather than the *Victoria* complete the circumnavigation of the globe. Magellan's flagship should have sailed back to Spain. But history does not always satisfy human wishes.

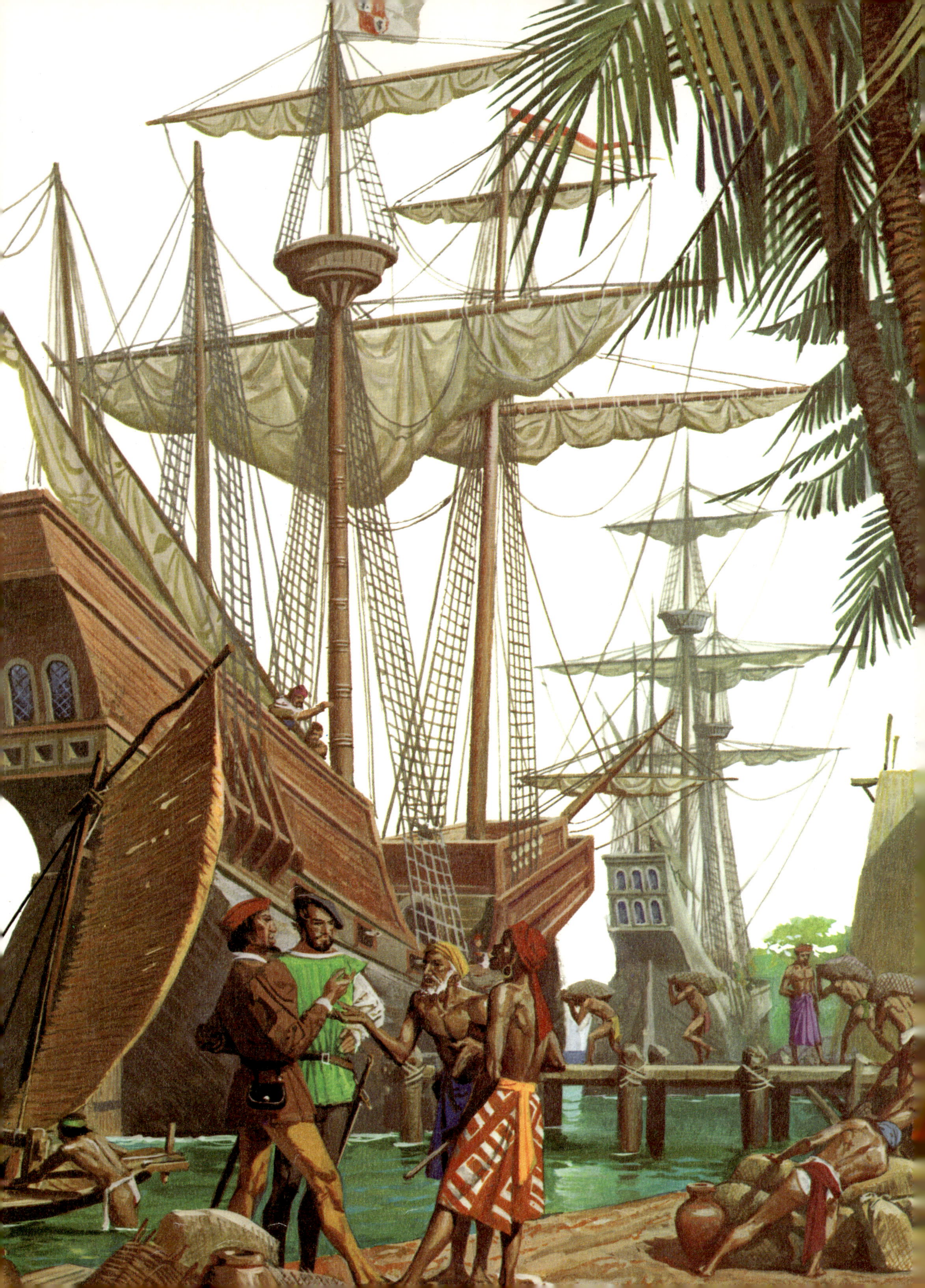

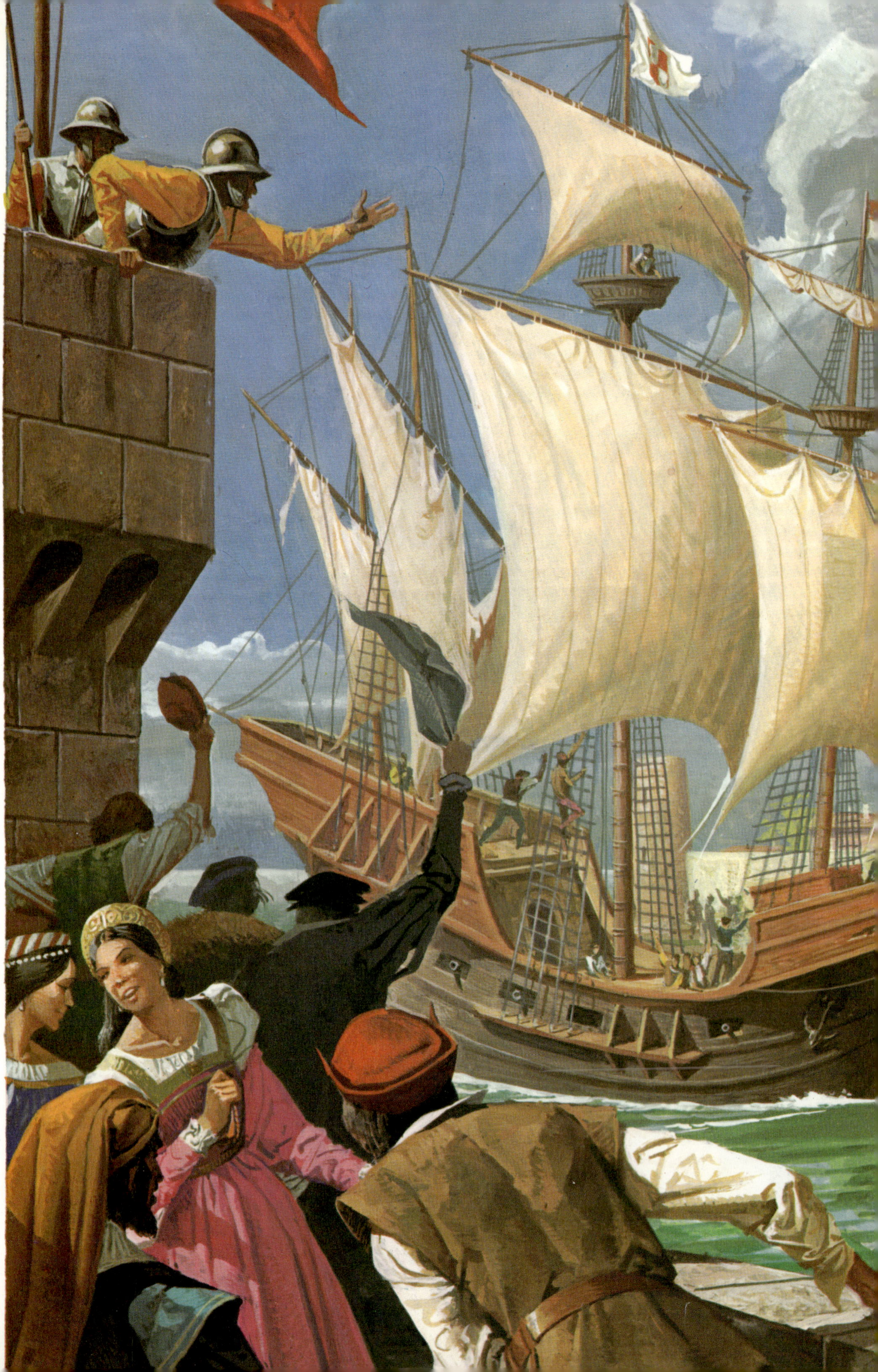

Only the Victoria remained of the five ships that had set out under Magellan's command. Her captain now was Juan Sebastian del Cano, a Spaniard chosen by the officers because he was the best navigator on board. Del Cano held to a course south from Tidore through the Malay Archipelago until he reached Timor in the Sunda Islands. After bartering for a final supply of food, he set out for the Indian Ocean.

The Victoria, a Spanish ship, could not follow the route north of Java to Malacca because the Portuguese would have seized her and interned her crew. Del Cano therefore turned south of Java into the open sea. His route involved a long, dangerous voyage across the Indian Ocean at its widest point in order to avoid Portuguese fleets.

"Death is better than a Portuguese prison," the Captain said to his men. "We must trust in God and ourselves to get us home."

Some of them did die in the Indian Ocean, the victims of hunger or disease. The rest suffered horribly. But Del Cano maneuvered his ship across to the southern tip of Africa, where he rounded the Cape of Good Hope.

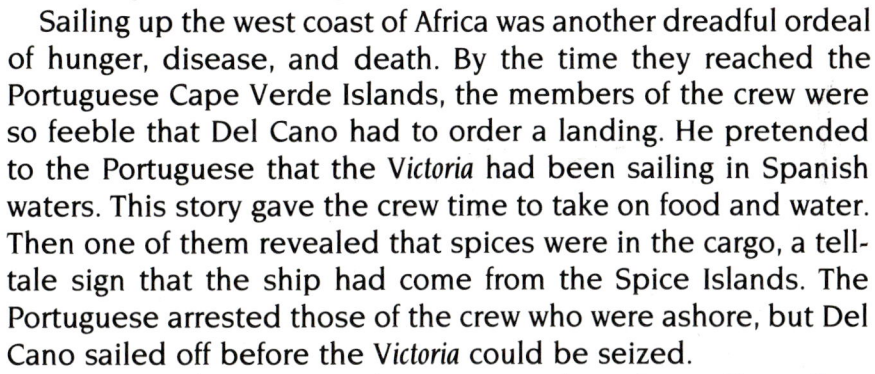

Sailing up the west coast of Africa was another dreadful ordeal of hunger, disease, and death. By the time they reached the Portuguese Cape Verde Islands, the members of the crew were so feeble that Del Cano had to order a landing. He pretended to the Portuguese that the Victoria had been sailing in Spanish waters. This story gave the crew time to take on food and water. Then one of them revealed that spices were in the cargo, a telltale sign that the ship had come from the Spice Islands. The Portuguese arrested those of the crew who were ashore, but Del Cano sailed off before the Victoria could be seized.

On September 6, 1522, the surviving ship of Magellan's fleet sailed into the harbor of San Lucar de Barrameda, from which she had departed nearly three years before. She carried eighteen men out of the hundreds who had left San Lucar aboard five ships on September 20, 1519.

Word of the return preceded the Victoria up the Guadalquiver, so an immense crowd greeted the Victoria when she reached Seville. There were loud cheers as the eighteen came ashore. Everyone wanted to meet them and hear of their adventures.

The Emperor Charles V summoned Del Cano to Valladolid. Pigafetta also went to the royal Court.

"Where is Magellan?" Charles asked.

"Magellan is dead, your Majesty," Del Cano replied.

Then Pigafetta explained how the commander of the expedition had lost his life in the Philippine Islands.

"Well, his name will live in history," said the Emperor.

Charles V was right. Magellan had said he would prove the world was round—and his ship the Victoria had proved it. Magellan's fame is that of the sea captain who made possible the first circumnavigation of the globe. He guided his ships westward from Spain to the Philippines. His spirit inspired those who guided the single ship westward from the Philippines to Spain. He deserves to be called the Great Circumnavigator.

The Death Of Ferdinand Magellan

When we reached land, those men had formed in three divisions to the number of more than one thousand five hundred persons. When they saw us, they charged down upon us with exceedingly loud cries, two divisions on our flanks and the other on our front. When the captain saw that, he formed us into two divisions, and thus did we begin to fight.

The musketeers and crossbowmen shot from a distance for about a half-hour, but uselessly; for the shots only passed through the shields which were made of thin wood and the arms (of the bearers). The captain cried to them, "Cease firing! Cease firing!" but his order was not heeded at all. When the natives saw that we were shooting our muskets to no purpose, crying out they determined to stand firm, for they redoubled their shouts.

When our muskets were discharged, the natives would never stand still, but leaped hither and thither, covering themselves with their shields. They shot so many arrows at us and hurled so many bamboo spears (some of them tipped with iron) at the captain-general, besides pointed stakes hardened with fire, stones, and mud, that we could scarcely defend ourselves.

Seeing that, the captain-general sent some men to burn their houses in order to terrify them. When they saw their houses burning, they were roused to greater fury. Two of our men were killed near the houses, while we burned twenty or thirty houses. So many of them charged down upon us that they shot the captain through the right leg with a poisoned arrow. On that account, he ordered us to retire slowly, but the men took to flight, except six or eight of us who remained with the captain. The natives shot only at our legs, for the latter were bare; and so many were the spears and stones that they hurled at us, that we could offer no resistance. The mortars in the boats could not aid us as they were too far away. So we continued to retire for more than a good crossbow flight from the shore, always fighting up to our knees in water.

The natives continued to pursue us, and picking up the same spear four or five times, hurled it again and again. Recognizing the captain, so many turned upon him that they knocked his helmet off his head twice, but he always stood firmly like a good knight, together with some others. Thus did we fight for more than one hour, refusing to retire further.

An Indian hurled a bamboo spear into the captain's face, but the latter immediately killed him with his lance, which he left in the Indian's body. Then, trying to lay hand on sword, he could draw it out but halfway, because he had been wounded in the arm with a bamboo spear. When the natives saw that, they all hurled themselves upon him. One of them wounded him on the left leg with a large cutlass, which resembles a scimitar, only being larger. That caused the captain to fall face downward, when immediately they rushed upon him with iron and bamboo spears, and also with their cutlasses, until they killed our mirror, our light, our comfort, and our true guide. When they wounded him, he turned back many times to see whether we were all in the boats.

Thereupon, beholding him dead, we, wounded, retreated, as best we could to the boats, which were already pulling off.

From the *Voyage* of Antonio Pigafetta

Antonio Pigafetta, Magellan's Diarist

Antonio Pigafetta was one of the eighteen men who circumnavigated the globe. He began the voyage aboard Magellan's flagship, the *Trinidad*. He finished it aboard the *Victoria*, the only ship of the fleet to complete the voyage envisioned by Magellan. His work, *The First Voyage Around the World*, is the best account of what happened along the way.

Pigafetta came from Vicenza in Venetian territory, where he was born about the year 1491. Little is known about him before 1519 when he sailed with Magellan. Because of his writing ability, Magellan assigned him to keep a diary of their time at sea. This diary was the basis of the book Pigafetta published after the *Victoria* returned to Spain.

His book is a moving tribute to Magellan, whom he calls "so noble a captain." It is also a valuable record of the islands and their inhabitants he saw in the East Indies.

The following passage, concerning one experience in the Philippine Islands, is a good example of his method:

Until the supper was brought in, the King with two of his chiefs and two of his beautiful women drank the contents of a large jar of palm wine without eating anything. I, excusing myself as I had supped, would only drink but once....

Then the supper, which consisted of rice and very salty fish, and served in porcelain dishes, was brought in. They ate their rice as if it were bread, which they cook in the following manner. They first put in an earthen jar like our jars, a large leaf which lines all of the jar. Then they add the water and rice, and after covering it, allow it to boil until the rice becomes as hard as bread, when it is taken out in pieces. Rice is cooked in the same way throughout those districts.

When we had eaten, the King had a reed mat and another of palm leaves, and a leaf pillow, brought in so that I might sleep on them. The King and his two women went to sleep in a separate place, while I slept with one of the chiefs.

When day came and until the dinner was brought in, I walked about the island. I saw many articles of gold in those houses but little food. After that, we dined on rice and fish, and at the conclusion of dinner, I asked the King by signs whether I could see the Queen.

He replied that he was willing, and we went together to the summit of a lofty hill, where the Queen's house was located. When I entered the house, I made a bow to the Queen, and she did the same to me, whereupon I sat down beside her. She was making a sleeping mat of palm leaves. In the house there were hanging a number of porcelain jars and four metal gongs—one of which was larger than the second, while the other two were still smaller—for playing upon. There were many male and female slaves who served her.

The Marianas, or the Islands of Thieves, as illustrated in the margin of Pigafetta's book. A typical Polynesian boat can be seen.

THE LUSIADS: A POEM ABOUT THE GREAT PORTUGUESE NAVIGATORS

Fifty years after Magellan's around-the-world voyage, Luis Vaz de Camoens wrote an epic poem celebrating Portugal as the mother of great navigators. He called his poem *The Lusiads*, meaning "The Sons of Lusus," the mythical founder of Portugal.

Camoens (1524-1580), born two years after the *Victoria* returned home, saw much of the growing Portuguese Empire. Like Magellan, he served in North Africa and India. He was in China, Southeast Asia, and East Africa. What he witnessed made him realize the tremendous feat of his fellow countrymen in discovering new lands, building forts and trading stations around the world, and controlling populations larger than that of Portugal itself.

Camoens had been aboard sailing ships buffeted by storms at the Cape of Good Hope and painfully sailed the Indian Ocean under a torrid sun. He had seen Portuguese viceroys governing strange peoples, Portuguese generals defeating native hordes, and Portuguese explorers pushing beyond the frontiers of the known world. The spectacle moved him to admiration and patriotism. He put both admiration and patriotism into *The Lusiads*, which he published in 1572. The following lines from his epic poem indicate how he felt about his homeland and its adventurers:

> Arms, and those matchless chiefs who from the shore
> Of Western Lusitania (Portugal) began
> To track the oceans none had sailed before,
> Yet past Tapróbané's (Sri Lanka's) far limit ran,
> And daring every danger, every war,
> With courage that excelled the powers of Man,
> Amid remotest nations caused to rise
> Young empire which they carried to the skies;
>
> So, too, good memory of those kings who went
> Afar, religion and our rule to spread;
> And who, through either hateful continent,
> Africa or Asia, like destruction sped;
> And theirs, whose valiant acts magnificent
> Saved them from the dominion of the dead,
> My song shall sow through the world's every part,
> So help me this my genius and my art....
>
> Love of country, thou shalt see, not dominated
> By vile reward but a deathless thing and high.
> My prize must not be basely estimated,
> Who still my native land would magnify.
> Hark and behold their glory celebrated,
> Whose lord thou art at height of sovranty,
> And thou shalt judge which is the better case,
> To rule the earth or govern such a race.

From *The Lusiads of Luiz de Camões*, translated by Leonard Bacon (The Hispanic Society of New York, 1950)

A fifteenth century print of *The Great Voyages* of Theodore de Bry. The ships from western countries sailed all the seas of the world in the Age of Discovery.

THE DIARY OF A GENOESE PILOT

There was a pilot from Genoa aboard Magellan's flagship, the *Trinidad*, who, like Pigafetta, kept a diary during the voyage. We are not sure of this pilot's name. The best guess is that he was Leone Pancaldo. His *Diary* is priceless because without it we would know little or nothing about the fate of the *Trinidad*, which was damaged in the Moluccas and could not sail with the *Victoria*. The men aboard the *Trinidad* tried, after repairing their ship, to return to Europe from the west. They hoped to retrace the outward voyage of Magellan's fleet, and to reach America by way of the Pacific.

It was a rash decision, leading to disaster. After a terrible voyage into the Pacific, the *Trinidad* had to return to the Moluccas with a crew decimated by starvation, thirst, and illness.

At the Moluccas, the Portuguese, under Antonio de Brito, imprisoned all the sailors. A few managed to escape and return to their homelands after many years. Among those, fortunately for us, was the Genoese pilot. Here is his passage on the end of the *Trinidad*:

They ran out of bread, wine, meat, and oil, and found themselves with only rice and water. The cold was intense and they had no proper clothing. The men began to die. When this happened, they decided to return to the Moluccas, and did so as quickly as they could. When they were still five hundred leagues away, they tried to land on the island of Magregua, but were unable to do so because it was night. They waited until the following morning, but still did not succeed. They then tried Dhomi and Batechina. When they had dropped their anchor, a boat came up containing several men, among whom was the chief of an island called Geilolo. He informed them that the Portuguese were building a fortress in the Moluccas.

When they learned this, they sent a boat with some men to the Portuguese commander, Antonio de Brito, to ask him to come and get their ship. They said that most of the crew were dead, the rest ill, and the ship could not be manned. When De Brito saw the message and looked at the map, he sent Garcia Amriquiz, captain of the San Giorgio, to look for the ship. When they found it, they brought it back to the fortress. While it was being unloaded, a storm blew in from the north and drove it onto the shore.

An old engraving of the *Victoria*, one of the five ships of Magellan's fleet. She was the only one to complete the mission and return home safely.

Historical Chronology

	Life of Magellan		Historical and Cultural Events
1480	Born of a noble country family in Portugal.	1488	The Portuguese navigator, Bartholomew Dias, rounds the Cape of Good Hope to East Africa.
		1492	Christopher Columbus lands in America on the island of Guanahani.
		1494	A new demarcation line between Spanish and Portuguese territory is established by the Treaty of Tordesillas.
		1497	John Cabot and his son, Sebastian, explore the coast of North America.
		1499	King Louis XII of France captures Milan and crosses Italy to Naples. He will be ousted by the Spaniards in 1504.
1505	Sails with an expedition under Francisco de Alameida; he is wounded in the Battle of Diu.	1505	Leonardo da Vinci works on his famous portrait, the Mona Lisa, also known as the "Giocanda."
1511	In the service of Alfonso de Albuquerque, he is present at the conquest of Malacca; he is made an officer for his bravery.	1508	Michelangelo begins the frescoes in the Sistine Chapel at the request of Pope Julius II.
1513	Repatriated to Lisbon because of hostility of his superiors; they resent his criticism.	1513	Niccolo Machiavelli writes *The Prince*, his masterpiece on political philosophy.

The departure of Magellan's fleet. A sixteenth century engraving.

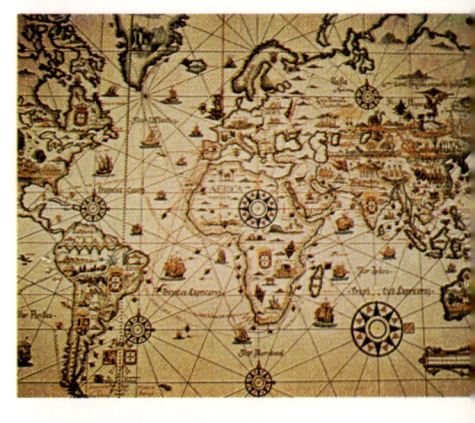

The subdivision of the globe according to the Treaty of Tordesillas. Oil on wood.

The entry of Louis XII into Naples. A fifteenth century miniature.

Leonardo da Vinci, the Mona Lisa, also the "Giocanda."

Life of Magellan	Historical and Cultural Events
1514 Sent as a soldier to Africa to fight against the Moors, and is wounded in the Battle of Azimur; he will limp for the rest of his life; returns to Lisbon to defend himself against the charge of having sold war-booty to the enemy; rehabilitated, he retires from public life and devotes himself to nautical and cosmographical study.	**1515** Francis I becomes king of France and wins the Battle of Marignano, giving him control of Milan; he will challenge Charles V, the Holy Roman Emperor, for supremacy in Italy, lose the Battle of Pavia (1525), and leave Charles triumphant.
1515 Encouraged by letters from his friend Francisco Serrão in the Moluccas, he conceives the idea of searching for a southwest passage from the Atlantic to the Pacific.	**1516** Sebastian Cabot accepts a commission from the King of Spain to explore in the direction of Hudson Bay.
1517 Discusses the idea with astronomer Ruy Faleiro, but King Manuel of Portugal refuses financial assistance, and he goes to Spain.	**1517** Martin Luther nails his 95 Theses on a church door in Wittenberg, the start of his break with the Catholic Church.
1518 Under the protection of the young King Charles I of Spain, and with financing from private interests, he is able to get his project underway.	
1519 Sets out from San Lucar de Barrameda on September 20 with a fleet of five ships: *Trinidad* (his flagship), *San Antonio*, *Concepcion*, *Victoria*, and *Santiago*.	**1519** Hernando Cortez, the cruel Spanish conqueror, lands in Mexico and in two years has wrested power from Montezuma in the Aztec Empire. Montezuma

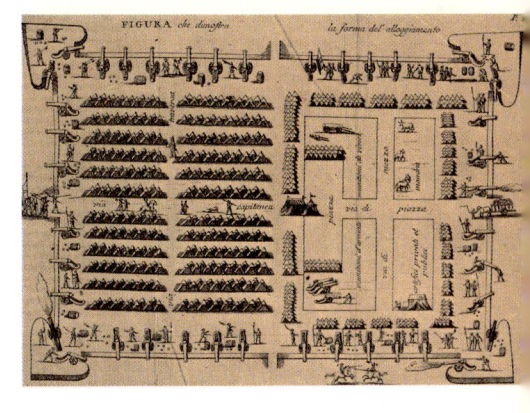

Niccolo Machiavelli, a chart from *The Art of War*.

Francis I, king of France, on horseback. Painted at the end of the sixteenth century.

A view of James Bay in the southern area of Hudson Bay.

Hernando Cortez at the Battle of Otumba in Mexico. Anonymous painting.

Life of Magellan	Historical and Cultural Events
	is killed by his own people as he attempts to head off a revolution.
1520 Having crossed the Atlantic and stopped briefly at Brazil, he reaches the River Plate on January 10. Arrives on March 31 at Port San Julian, where he spends the winter; the *Santiago* is lost while exploring the coast. He suppresses a mutiny among his captains; the *San Antonio* abandons the fleet and returns to Spain. He discovers the strait leading from the Atlantic into the Pacific on October 21; it is now called the Strait of Magellan. He and his men notice the star formations now called the Clouds of Magellan.	**1520** Raphael dies, only 37 years old; his most important paintings include portraits of Julius II and Leo X, the Sistine Madonna, and the Madonna of the Cardellino. Charles V is crowned Holy Roman Emperor.
1521 After a harrowing voyage across the Pacific, he reaches the Marianas and the Philippines. He lands on a number of islands in the name of the king of Spain, imposes a tribute, and has some local people baptized. Leaders on the island of Mactan reject his demands. He leads a landing party, and is killed in a skirmish on April 27.	**1521** Martin Luther is condemned by the Diet of Worms after being excommunicated by Pope Leo X. He seeks refuge with Frederick of Saxony, and begins a German translation of the Bible. Emperor Charles V condemns Luther, and forbids the distribution of his writings.

The Strait of Magellan and the Land of the Giants. A map by Sebastian Munster.

Raphael, the Madonna of the Cardellino.

Raphael, Pope Leo X with Cardinals.

Titian, portrait of the Emperor Charles V.

Life of Magellan	Historical and Cultural Events
	The Ottoman Empire under Suleiman I, "The Magnificent," reaches the height of its power. It extends beyond the Danube to Belgrade. King Manuel I, "the Fortunate," of Portugal dies. During his reign, voyages of exploration reached Brazil and the East Indies.
1522 The *Victoria* returns to San Lucar on September 6. Under Sebastian del Cano, she has crossed the Indian Ocean and rounded the Cape of Good Hope—a practical demonstration that the earth is a sphere. European cartographers draw up new maps of the world, using information from this voyage. The size of the Pacific Ocean is recognized for the first time.	**1522** Ulrich Zwingli publishes two tracts attacking the Catholic Church. They give momentum to the Reformation in Switzerland.
1523 Pigafetta, using his notes from aboardship, writes his *The First Voyage Around the World*, giving a graphic account of Magellan and his achievement.	**1526** Saint Ignatius Loyola writes his *Spiritual Exercises*, which become the basic religious book of the Jesuits. Babur founds the Mogul Empire in India.
	1527 Henry VIII asks the Pope for the annulment of his marriage to Catherine of Aragon in order to legalize his relationship with Anne Boleyn. When the Pope refuses, he severs all relations with the Catholic Church.

Amber in Jaipur, India, the Temple of Jagat Shromani or Vishnu. Mogul architecture.

The beach at Mactan where Magellan was killed.

A view of the Cape of Good Hope, rounded by the *Victoria* on its voyage home.

Henry VIII of England, portrait by Holbein.

Books for Further Reading

The Explorers by Richard Humble,
Time-Life Books, 1978.

The First Men Around the World by Andrew Langley,
Silver Burdett, 1982.

Ferdinand Magellan: Noble Captain by Katherine Wilkie,
Houghton-Mifflin, 1963.

Magellan's Voyage Around the World: Three Contemporary Accounts
edited by Charles E. Nowell,
Northwestern University Press, 1962.